# Alien God

## Michael Maher

# Dedication

Dedicated to my children and to those that I have
loved and lost in my life.

# Table of Contents

# Acknowledgement

I would like to thank JoAnne Howard for her inspiration.

Special thank you to Sydney and Jake Wolfe for the artwork and illustration.

Thank you, Mr. and Mrs. Nelson, for helping with editing and formatting.

# Introduction

At the beginning of the pandemic period, information about anything and everything, was coming at us from all directions. My normal attention to news on mainstream outlets had been at best, in a mode of half-listening. I had even less interest in Politics, that seemed to be getting worse and more divisive than ever. So, I only started to listen, to pay attention, as they started the talk about the rising Corona virus cases in Europe, particularly, in Italy. I was not satisfied with the news on national outlets and so began to spend more time researching. I had spent several years prior, doing genealogy research on my family lines, so was accustomed to doing searches and as the days went by, I discovered many new journalistic media sources, with a wide range of topics, opinions, facts and other support data. What started out as research about the virus, became research on EVERYTHING!

I started to feel my way around in the "sea" of mixed information and to find any that I thought would be helpful tidbits. As these many videos, interviews, statements, reports, other sources of data presented themselves to me, I gleaned all I thought to be helpful and committed much to my memory. I felt like I was a "filter." I was pouring it all through my eyes, ears and my heart, then making the choice to discard it or add it to the other accumulated wisdom and opinions I already had stored in my mind.

This journey became my path to truth. This is my story of my surprising introduction to a world I had not considered, but had in all my previous lifetime, been introduced to many of these same themes. I had been raised to believe in God, the Bible, that we have both good and evil here on earth. I heard of strange happenings throughout history, with encounters with many odd beasts, the possibility of life on other planets, flying saucers, trips to the moon and other off world travel in space and many strange things that cannot be explained or connected and do not have anything to do with one another what so ever. Or do they?

See how my curiosity helped find answers that fit the puzzle, that existed in my heart and what led me to find a surprising connection to our Heavenly Father.

# Chapter 1
# Questions for God

We had been corresponding through emails for about 6 months.  I had posed many questions to Johanne about what she had written in her book and on her blogs.

One day, she asked what we would ask God if we could ask directly, anything about anything and what of the Archangels? She said it would be a lot of work for her to ask for us, but wanted to for our family.

I brought the question to my wife.  We discussed it and had some ideas. We also asked my wife's daughter, Katherine, if she had any questions she would like to ask.  Between us, we came up with a list and I emailed

Johanne back with our questions or comments. I also told her of a recent event that my wife's daughter had shared with us, about her own daughter.

Katherine is a woman in her mid-thirties and has four children now. She is very prayerful and routinely participates in or leads Bible studies with other young adults. She teaches her children, to be kind, caring and God loving individuals.

One day, she was returning from a trip to the store, when she noticed the flashing emergency lights and heard the siren of an ambulance coming up quickly behind them. She pulled to the side of the road to let the emergency vehicle pass. Katherine had three of her children with her at the time. JoJo, the three-year-old, became very concerned and asked if there were people in there that were hurt, to which her mother replied, that there probably were. The little one then asked her mom, can we pray for them? Katherine said that they could and asked if she would lead them. JoJo did and asked that Jesus take care of those who were hurt.

My wife, Nana, as she is affectionately called by her grandchildren, asked how she could be used by God, to help others. Her daughter Katherine asked questions about why God doesn't speak to us directly and had other questions about Jesus' death. She also wondered why God hadn't defeated sin and death and things of that nature. I made the point that I really didn't want to ask questions if I were able to speak to

God directly, I wanted a chance to see my son again, who had died many years before in an accident and that I missed him more than any other human I had known in my life.

After a few days, Johanne returned with her answers in an email. She had much to report.

*"First, the seeing of his son Matthew (J: Is your son named Matthew?), he is with us and he will serve many evident truths with his father soon because the meeting time opens to many and all good souls. His son opens to many with us and heals many with truth and greater renewals of knowledge on Earth. He is (like) a teacher who will share many good ways learned with us, and many love him here. Tell Mike that his son will return to Earth with us because this helps answer serving for all. This will open Mike's heart to more coming truths."*

*"Tell Nana she will be very important in the renewing of health by way of learning for children and these ways of care for the injured ones. Be certain she understands my words as she knows she has a gift for this. And her daughter will renew with evidence of greater truth than seen on Earth, because she will open to the ways beliefs are changed, better seeing truth and renewing this with many others. And know her daughter (J: your grand-daughter) will renew with the evident truth of beliefs in our laws. Our laws are unknown beliefs on Earth and will flourish in time, and so this child will serve with great integrity and power of truth.*

*And more, these words of knowledge I share are mostly for this family, as they are my children in evidence of their pure hearts and good will. I am pleased and proud of them and well seeing they open to me and my ways.*

*All beliefs of truth will open more truths and knowledge, and all is well coming. Be ready."*

Upon reading this, I got "choked up" and started to get teary eyed. I was confused about the name Matthew for my son. The message was very clearly answering our questions.

The email went on to add,

*"Knowledge opens to many, but not to all people on Earth. Arrivals will be better understood by my children who are waiting for my renewed return to Earth, and the return of my son Jesus who returns with us and many others exploding the truth visited by the words in the Bible. But my words are not all in this book. Some are truths and some answer to the serving of Rome only. This needs to be understood, and because many as said are serving deceptions, I can only use my children to open to these times, those who are listening.*

*Soon this will be seen and those who are dealing with us will evidently share knowledge of our coming to Earth. And this is what is needed to free our children from continual bondage and serious abuses of their bodies and souls, in evidence of these days of responding to poisoning my children, to change their souls and marking them with the sign of Lucifer and his demons.*

*Answers are coming, be ready and see this be soon."*
*God*

I responded to Johanne with our many thanks and said that I needed to tell her the story of my son.  I went on to write:

*My son's name was Shane.  He was my first born.  He died in a motorcycle accident when he was 18 years old, just a few weeks short of finishing high school.  He was a troubled soul, much caused by the divorce of his parents and the cancer his sister was stricken with at age 12 (But has survived).  He had a heart of gold but his behavior was sometimes, mischievous.  He did poorly in school as soon as the life events happened.  He found alcohol and drugs.  His friends loved him.  His teachers who struggled with him, but loved him somehow, oddly enough.  They had nothing bad to say about his character, just his work.  His death was my absolute low point in my life.  To take another breath was so hard.  I actually told myself to breathe.  Days, weeks, months then years, passed.  Memories fade.  His funeral was well attended.  The funeral director said there were 600 that fit in the church, another 100 or so had to stand outside.  As my ex-wife, my daughter and my son's girlfriend and I followed the casket to the front of the church, my ex's husband was walking slightly behind us and my ex seemed confused in her grief and didn't know who to turn to for support. She outreached her hand, almost flailing towards me, so I stepped closer and put my arm around her and helped her get to the front pew. She was also at the bottom of her feelings. During the service, the priest, (who was of Irish decent much like my family) spoke highly of Shane and told us all to remember his big Irish grin. The grin was his trademark. It is why people were drawn to him. The priest also said to us all, "Imagine he was on a ship and we see the ship fading away over the horizon and that we are all sad to see him go but to remember, where he arrives, they are greatly excited that he is finally coming to be with them. The cemetery was greatly crowded with people when the priest arrived to give gravesite rites. When that was done, things and days moved quickly and soon the hard day I had ended by saying good bye to family and friends who were going home.*

*Fast forward from 1994 to 2014. The company I worked for, was celebrating our jubilee. We had many events, including a trip for 1500 employees to the Bahamas (for which I had the honor of planning all the travel arrangements). One event was a picnic for the employees, family members and company board members. One of the board members happened to be the priest from the funeral and now was known as "Monsignor." I had bumped in to him several times over the years and would have only short conversations and "HI, bye" kind of moments. So, he's at this* picnic. I'm walking around being social, including a couple moments of speaking with him and other board members. About 15 minutes later, my aunt, who also had worked for our company, came to me urgently and said, "Michael, Monsignor is frantically looking for you and would like a word with you". Now, he was about 85 at the time, so very old. I found him and he pulled me aside and he started to explain to me that he was truly sorry for what he had done and asked for my forgiveness. He explained that he had finished the burial rites for my son and realized there were so many people coming to the burial, that half were still walking to the grounds when he had finished and this had so bothered him all these years and it haunted him. He broke into tears and cried. I hugged him and told him to "please, don't worry about that. That was so long ago. Please do not think about this anymore. It's okay." We parted ways and we never spoke again. He died this last year. I did nothing but read his obituary.

I don't know why the name "Matthew" unless it was who he was in another lifetime. He was Shane, Shaner, Shaner Baner, my little man, etc., but never Matthew. Your messages have been very comforting and I fully expect to play some role as we move towards this change. I look forward to all that has been told to us.

Thank you so much and I truly appreciate the blessings you have brought us in so many ways.

This exchange happened mid-August of 2021. A couple of days later, Johanne directed me to go look up the meaning of the name Matthew and the name Shane. When I did, I found they have the same meaning. It is "Gift of God." Now I was understanding.

So much had transpired since my wife and I had watched the video the first time.

# Chapter 2
# It's Going to be Biblical

It was late December of 2020 and the whole world was in utter chaos. Rioting, election issues, Covid-19 pandemic, crazy people everywhere. I was so glad I had retired 5 years before. Because of restrictions and just trying to be careful and stay away from people in general, I was spending more time on my computer, researching my family history. When that got to be too much or I would hit a brick wall, I would switch gears and start reading as much as I could on everything happening in the world. One video or story would lead me to another, to another and then probably, another! Because of my genealogy work and my work habits of my career, I had honed my attention to detail and my ability to "collect" information in my memory and easily recall it. As I started my gleaning of facts and factoids, commonality in different subjects were noticed; opinions and beliefs were being challenged, dissected and reassembled; things started to be rearranged in mind and strong opinions began forming. I formulated new opinions that differed from old, some I had been aligned with my whole life.

As I went from one topic to another, one particular evening I saw a video on a *Bitchute* channel, SGTreports. It was a site I had visited on other occasions and it had a new video titled, *"What comes next is Biblical. Literally."*

That video title piqued my interest, so I started listening to the 45-minute segment. The interviewer, Sean, was speaking to Johanne Howard, the author of a recently published book, "The Wisdom of God: *God calls on his Children"*. They talked on a variety of current events such as the pandemic, elections and general moral decay going on around us. About the midway point in the interview, even though Sean had made mention of the book Johanne had written, they had not said much about it. After about 11 minutes in, she said something about when she started to "receive" and then I really started to listen. She explained herself quite well about her reluctance to believe what was happening to her, as she was getting messages and conversations with these entities. She certainly did not think she was worthy if these contacts were indeed Angels. Johanne explained how a job she had worked in as a teacher had started to reveal to her that there was evil in the organization and they were becoming aggressive towards her, knowing she was a good soul. She was contacted after writing a poem to God, in which she was pleading for help or assistance. As I listened, she got to a part where she explained that people in general do not understand God and the Angels. Most probably think of them as ghosts or spirits floating around on a cloud or something, when in reality, they are real beings and are like us. They have come back to reclaim Earth from Lucifer, who took it after a battle was fought and now God and his army have returned to end Lucifer's reign. She spoke of Universal Laws that the rest of the universe follows and that our Ten Commandments are only some of those laws. The main "rule" of these laws is the guidance to "CAUSE NO HARM." And that they cannot intervene or interfere with any civilization that doesn't ask for help. They can however, intervene if total annihilation of a planet may happen, as would be the case if a nuclear war started here on Earth. This is what they are waiting for, to make a move. This story is easily found as written about in the book of Revelation, in the Holy Bible.

After I listened to the video, I went out of the room and found my wife and told her she needed to hear this. She was also amazed. Nana is a very kind and generous, caring soul herself, so this really resonated with her. She understood. She also believed. I listened carefully a couple more times and then told my wife that I had to find this book.  After much searching, it finally dawned on me to try Amazon and there it was. I ordered it and was so happy when it came a few days later.  I was so excited to read this.

# Chapter 3
# Reading is Difficult

I began to read the book the evening I received it. In reading the Introduction, I learned how she started down this path that began in 2003, when she started to "receive" messages from the Spiritual world. In 2012 she started posting these messages on her blog site. People from all over the world started seeing these words and became interested. They started asking questions and they were given answers. Unknowingly, I had happened across these messages myself sometime during those days, but did not realize it until I had read this book. Then I suddenly recalled seeing this. The reason I did not spend much time there was that it was unconventional wording and I was having trouble reading it and making sense of the content.

Now all these years later, I understand the journey from then until now.

As described in the book and later in emails shared with Johanne, she explained that in the start of her communications, the language was different and she had to learn the meaning of some of the words being used. She recognized the style to be close to Sanskrit, a 3500-year-old language. Her career of teaching, specifically French at the high school level and general language knowledge was very helpful to understand what was being told to her.

The first part of the book was easy to read and it was quickly understood that this was God speaking. There did not seem to be any trouble reading that part. I learned later that when she was instructed to write this part, that God had gone from using a more ancient dialog to a more modern sounding message. Part one of the book was God's opening messages on a variety of topics that the reader could understand how all things have come to be and what they are going to do now to change it. It was an introduction to who God is and clarifies the understanding of the evil we have all been subjected to for thousands of years.

As I moved into the messages from the blogs and tried to read it, I struggled so much I had to start over repeatedly. I tried reading it fast, I tried reading it out loud. I took a break and let my wife try to read it. That did not go well. She decided that I needed to read it to her and I did that a couple of times but it was not making sense. I could tell some of the words used could have so many different meanings. I even used replacement words for some used in the book and that helped, but because some words can have multiple meanings, it did not always fit the sentence. I gave up several times and would dive into it again, trying to power my way through it. I was determined to read it and understand it. Then I tried something else. Some sentence reminded me of how a Russian accent would sound saying those words. In 2002, I had taken a 5-day trip to Russia and the few people I spoke with there would say words in English with that accent. That accent was remembered and I applied it to these words as I read them. Soon I was reading at a good speed and that opened me to reading it normally, as time passed.

The messages were often slightly repetitive so I got into the habit of reading until I found something that had already been said, then I jumped to the next sentence or paragraph. Later that became an issue as I must have skipped content that was different. What happened in the end when I finally finished it, as I tried to recall what I just had digested, the feeling came over me that I had not done a good job of getting the message as intended.

After a couple of weeks, I decided I needed to take notes. I gathered pen and paper and began reading for the second time, this time making notes of significant statements. That was a good thing. But when I finished the book the second time and reviewed my notes, intending to use them as my reference to go back and read specific chapters or paragraphs, I discovered that I missed things again. This was repeated at least 4 times. Still, to this day, I will read a chapter and learn something new or a small missed detail. It is so amazing.

# Chapter 4
# First Communications

After the book was published, Johanne had started a new online blog. She began posting content in mid-December of 2020. Having read the book and made notes, I was ready to learn more. I noticed she had included a contact page and welcomed comments and questions

The book had contained a few chapters where God answered questions that readers had for a period of time. Some examples were people asking what they (God and the Angels/Archangels) looked like, why haven't they come yet, when are they coming and similar queries. After reading the book, I had my own questions. As I discussed these with my wife, she encouraged me to just ask. I was hesitant because I was afraid. Yes, afraid that if this was all real, then I might make myself more visible and what if I had not lived my life as God had wished me to?  I was afraid of being noticed.

One day I decided to go with a few questions that were not too "deep" and wrote them on her blog site.  She responded soon after on February 19, 2021.  I had asked her about the language used and commented on how difficult it was to read.  I also asked questions about DNA, who God's direct children are and a bit about Sophia, which was significant information about an entity that was unknown to me before this book. The body of the email is provided here, as it contains numerous important pieces of a what I would describe as a "puzzle" that I was trying to assemble in my heart and mind.

> *Dear Mike,*
>
> *Thank you for your questions. I welcome all your questions and I will try to answer them to the best of my understanding.*
>
> *The language is difficult because the phrases organized are from a language related to Sanskrit. For example, the word 'setu' means bridging but it also means reunion, reuniting, reunification and maybe more. The language is condensed in meaning and the meaning comes from the context. But as you read on in part 2 and part 3, you will find that this improves. When I began receiving the language it was very archaic (like Shakespeare is to us now). Gabriel is much better at*

*current English, he helped to make connections, and I noticed uses of expressions like "here is the thing ... " entered in our communications. The use of language is fascinating as it evolves, and of course they can speak very good French, Spanish, Latin and probably all languages with an 'accent'. Having taught both French and English to international students for many years, it was easier for me to unravel what was meant, and of course there was an adaptation that took place with practice. I recorded over 100 words from their language that we also use to communicate.*

*DNA. God said that blood is everything. It holds all the information of the being's lives. The soul is the seat (in the heart), the center of the person (or animal). It holds all the memories of past lives and of the place of emergence. It comes to Earth, incarnates and is born into a new life. It comes with the knowledge of many previous life experiences and is unique because of the soul, the seed that ignites and enters life. (I am French Catholic from many generations, yet my Catholic training is different from English Catholics. One difference is the mention of reincarnation.)*

*The spirit is the energy vibration or the auric field. (Dr. Valerie Hunt's studies from UCLA explains this well. It is measurable with instruments.) We can see how this energy affects its surroundings, like a happy person coming into a room making others happy. The spirit is unseen but can be felt. Also, a spirit is a missing person, not there but we know they exist, like the Holy Spirit. God tells us in his words that the Holy Spirit of the Trinity is his missing wife Sophia taken by Lucifer.*

*God tells me that his direct children are Jesus (Teacher), Gabriel, Micheal, Uriel, Raphael, Sauriel, and Jeremiel. (The names may be spelt differently in different religions). Their DNA was stolen by Lucifer who made other beings, as this is what Lucifer did on Earth. Sophia discovered this travesty and tried to stop Lucifer and so she adopted all the children in the result of this to save them. Some were changed into beasts and God kept these ones with him until their death. Sophia eventually was taken by Lucifer. This was the time of the great wars. (See the hieroglyphs of Giza).*

*I understand how this information can be very difficult for some to accept. It was not in my life's plan to do this. I was contacted to help open the way for God to reunite with all his children. I cannot say if all humans are from God because Lucifer went from place to place collecting DNA to make his own world. He copies; he does not create. And I do not know about the Ancient ones but I will ask today during prayer.*

*I hope this information was useful to you. I am very happy to answer your questions anytime.*

*Be one with God and be well.*

*Johanne Howard*

My question about the Ancient ones, was from something I read in the book that surprised me.

> *"God loves his children.  Know that I am your Father and your Creator and there is no one else above me but our Ancient Ones who are our caring loves.  They are always with us to help with our plans and our renewals, as we too open to evolution and better renewals of who we are and as we better open to others.  Believe answers are here for you.  Believe you will be very pleased when we become as one to respond together to our guiding principles of the Universal Laws."*

(J. Howard, *The Wisdom of God,* 2020, p25)

As with other questions I came to ask about things in the book, Johanne did not always know the reason something was written and explained that she only wrote what she received and did not question or try to put her "spin" on meanings.  Almost as if it went from God's mouth, through the tip of her pencil and on to the paper.   The ensuing questions and answers were to say the very least, most interesting!

# Chapter 5
# The Ancient Ones

Johanne posted on her blog on February 28, 2021 the following:

*For Mike: The Ancient Ones. I do not know about the Ancient Ones written in the book but I asked for clarification (Feb.19). This is what I asked and the response I received. Q. Can you share about the Ancient Ones, who they are, what is their purpose and where they live? A. Be certain these questions can be visited by us. Be understanding us by understanding the Ancient Ones. They are seen as parents to us. They are seeing to all questions, are responding and they live in a dimension different from ours. Be understanding how we are better answered by them as they tell us who opens to whom, and they are also like us in many ways with telepathy and greater evidence of truth. They are in body as we are but renew with great seeings, knowledge and truth. They ask us all to be united under the Universal Laws and we honor them with belief of who they are and only as the ones who open to everything in all places.    Be certain these words are unknown on Earth and many are believing that none is above God, but the truth be told the Ancient Ones are above all seeings of all planets and peoples. Q. Where did the Ancient Ones emerge from? A. They were as I am and now they are the Ancient Ones as I will be in time, a very long time. And know these are many times to come but seeing a short life on Earth, these answers are eternity and infinite. And soon you will see these ways yourselves in evidence of the coming renewals.*

I was thrilled to read those words.  I quickly wrote Johanne an email and thanked her:

*Johanne,*

*Thank you.  I did see your statement on the blog/website.  The answer is intriguing.  I have decided I need to read your book again as only more questions seem to come to mind and I'm afraid I might have missed something or misunderstood some statements.  There is also an internal struggle I feel with my own faith.  Oddly enough, with what I have read in your book, I look at many other subjects differently and have some soul searching to do. I have to sort these things out but want you to know I am very appreciative that you responded to my initial questions, to help in my search for understanding.*

*Mike Maher*

Now that I had "broken the ice" and started asking my questions, I began to make a list of what things were really making me take notice and what was driving me to know more.

# Chapter 6
# Significant Questions

Johanne's book was quickly making me review and rethink most of my beliefs and understandings. But I was ready and willing to take a different look at everything. I was open to looking at these new truths, comparing to my beliefs, analyzing all that was being presented and coming to new conclusions. Some of the entries in the book that I took note of and used in my next questions to her were:

*"On the day of our arrivals, you will see many lights in the sky and many visits will begin to open to our children first, and settling with our reunions. All others will be visited, renewing with their families, as they are on their way to meet with them.*

*Be patient as we cannot all arrive at the same time, and we will need many places to land our ships. Airports, sports complexes and fields of hay will better serve our many different ships. These ships are only better seen by some of you now but soon will be seen by all."*

J. Howard, *The Wisdom of God,* 2020, p25)

*"The Mother has long denied her role of the Archai Omega, because of her pain in her heart. She is the one who is the bride of God. She is the one that wills turmoil and torment with her sufferings, but she does not know it.*

*This awakening is coming now, and she is understanding it. You must open to her and trust that she can heal, and that her healing is your healing, and to the way of your freedom from torment and turmoil, and heal all that stops you from coming home to my love."*

(J. Howard, *The Wisdom of God,* 2020, p17)

*"Be ready to answer to our call as all seeing will open to you and answer many more questions that you will ask. Be certain we are coming very soon as the wars erupt in the Middle East and open to the way for our arrivals. Now see these words as you may but know all heals after these first attacks. Soon many more will*

*answer to our call as we arrive to settle these actions against humans of Earth.*

*As we arrive, all armaments will be disabled and not one artillery weapon will be used against anyone. Be serving these understandings as we will help all renew without wars and we heal answers to all false wars said to be in the interest of democracy or Islamic beliefs. All will be dealt with and all will be ended by us, as these constructs are not of my words and never were"*

(J. Howard, *The Wisdom of God,* 2020, p118)

I prepared another email with several new questions and sent it to Johanne for her responses.

On April 14, 2021, I sent the following:

*Johanne,*

*Hoping this doesn't get too long! I have more questions after rereading your book. I took lots of notes and hope that if I gather my thoughts properly, I may be able to have an intelligent conversation with others if the chance arises. I already took a slight chance by discussing with my 14-year-old granddaughter, what would it look like if God suddenly came to Earth. Without saying too much, I told her that God is probably from space and if we suddenly saw lots of ships in the air, we should not be scared and we may find out it is God and his Army. It was a good discussion and I made sure she wasn't starting to think her grandpa was going off the deep end!!*

*My initial question is for you to answer as I just wonder how their first contact with you went. Did you hear a voice or did you just have a "thought" that seemed silly or not something you would think? I am trying to imagine if it were a clear voice or a distant sounding voice as heard.*

*Next, I thought I read that God said Jesus became human, with the help of Gabriel and without God's knowledge or permission, but I cannot find that comment again and I don't think I just dreamed that. Do you know which chapter I should look in, if it is there? And in reading the few comments God makes about the death of Jesus on the cross and his "disgust" with the displaying of the Crucifixes, my wife was wondering if we should be making the sign of the cross as a show of reverence anymore?*

*Another odd thought I had was about Sophia and the lack of any mention of Mary. Most "apparitions" that have been recorded, seem to all be assumed to be Mary, mother of Jesus but your book claims Sophia to be the mother of God's Children. The Fatima story in your book, identifies Sophia as the one that gave the secrets to the three children. Sophia is often mentioned in your book as the Holy Spirit or Mother. If you could explain the Mary/Sophia connection? There are also "secrets" that are connected to the Medjugorje apparitions that mysteriously stopped when the world-wide pandemic was announced.*

*Question about the great war that God and his Angels were attacked and had to run away. What kind of weapons would scare these beings to fear and run?*

*Lastly, most of what is written in your book about the event that brings God and his Angel army to Earth is about an atomic bomb in either, the middle east, North Korea to the US or Syria. With the time frame of 2012-2013, those were real threats but, Trump diffused the NK connection, found ways to ease tensions in the Middle East and accomplish some peace treaties, and put an end to Syrian (mostly) issues with eliminating ISIS. I read that God had to restrain from taking action to allow for Earthly resolution to some of these issues. There is almost no news anymore that is believable, so it is hard to know what kind of turmoil exists around the world these days, when all that is discussed, is Pandemic news.*

*With Trump's recent message about how he was instrumental in bringing the vaccines to the world, I now have reason to doubt he is on the side of good either! With no talk of war to speak of, and the crazy things being done worldwide to all people, how does a world event happen with weapons, if all that is being done is just to put people in bondage/slavery by one method or another. I see the evil escalate at a faster and faster rate each week. It's almost like evil is trying to take over just as fast as possible so that no other like Trump, can stop them. God said he needed the bomb devastation, to be able to come to Earth to interrupt Lucifer's plan. If we are all just being terrorized by other things, what brings God to end it?*

*Thank you so much for your time!*

*Mike Maher*

As a side note, the same things I mentioned in April of 2021 about war, has repeated itself over 5 years later and all of that was relayed in messages to Johanne in 2012-2013. Talks of peace, war in the middle east and many of the same issues then, are issues now.

Johanne answered me with her response the next day, on April 15th.

*Good morning, Mike,*

*I will do my best to answer your questions. These are excellent questions.*

**First paragraph questions.** *My first contact was through the use of a pendulum. I taught myself to use a pendulum and a chart. I read many books on the subject and was inspired to try it. I remembered my parents using a dowser to find water to dig a well. I used charts, as some naturopaths do, to find better cures for health* *problems. The pendulum was very active in my hand so I made an alphabetical chart and this became my telephone line. It took prayer, focus and discernment to navigate this communication tool. Then Uriel the Archangel opened to me first. (See Enoch 21:3 and Esdras 4:10-11, both are Apocryphal texts). He spoke in another language, then eventually in English and French. He governs over Earth and he spoke to me in preparation of the coming times. Then came Micheal, Raphael (briefly) and Gabriel who guided my re-education. Then Gabriel told me I was to be instructed by God because much needed to be said, and I speak to Gabriel occasionally although he is very busy now with the arrival preparations.*

*So, the messages are specific, spelt out letter by letter, this is important to me to get the message right.*

**Second Paragraph questions.** *"Thou shalt not make unto thee a graven image ..."*

*My house had crucifixes in every room until I understood that having an image of Jesus' tortured body was an assault and a threat to those who love him. (See the horrific depictures of Jesus on the cross and worst in the Vatican). The thinking behind this is: "If you do not obey, you will suffer this." And " You are guilty of his sufferings, bow down to this image, this is your guilt ". All this to me is cult talk as well as the other cult practices from all religions. God did not ask for this, the churches did. I now have a crucifix with a dove descending to Earth on it as a reminder.*

*God did not accept what Jesus did because it harmed him and allowed the Romans to do more harm to good people. Sophia is the Mother of the Archangels and God is their Father. She was taken by Lucifer and tortured in horrific ways until she lost herself in reincarnations and was not able to reconnect with her husband and children. Her soul was damaged and she never knew who she was through her incarnations. All her lives she died murdered, before she could figure out her truth. Before she was taken by Lucifer, she left a book for God and the Archangels to find. It is called 'Answers to answer', and Gabriel was given this book by the Ancient ones (I think), he then gave it to God. God originally thought that she left him. She did leave God in order to protect the children she adopted on Earth, but Lucifer killed many of them and blamed her for this. Gabriel and Jesus wanted to save her, they did not consult God. She was born as Mary. And Jesus was also tortured in horrific ways. I believe Sophia/ Mary is living incarnated on Earth now.*

### Third question. The great wars.

*Mars, the moon and Earth. Mars was inhabited by a great civilization. Earth was a creation of God and Sophia, it was their home. The war came with the attacks from these beings of darkness who came first as friends, neighbors and collaborators.*

*They destroyed Mars with powerful weapons and then arrived in very great numbers to take Earth, as this was their plan from the start. Their ship is the moon. These demons had interest in the knowledge known to God and Sophia. Lucifer is only capable of copying and repeating, he cannot 'create' anything more than repeated chaos (as we see today).*

*So, God was fighting a war with his army above Earth but could not return to Earth. He went out into the Universes to find allies, many of them suffered the same wars with these renegade demons. The Archangels managed to trap these demons on Earth (Earth is quarantined and cut off from other planets), sacrificing their planet to grow in strength and return in time. Now these people from different planets are united and form a formidable army. Now is the time. (Also see 'Paradise Lost' by Milton).*

***Fifth paragraph.*** *Book of Revelations: First there will be peace brokered then war will come. Yes, God refrains from taking action to allow Humans to better understand evil and their slavery.*

*God said to me that Trump served him, but that may mean different things. Trump did move the emotions of many people to open to the truth of tyranny that lives everywhere on Earth. Yet people are lining up for experimental gene changing 'vaccines' like lemmings going off a cliff. Moreover, we are seeing a division of souls, neighbor against neighbor, brother against brother and family and businesses taking political stances. People who we trusted are showing themselves to be something different, this is a necessary step for understanding.*

*It may not be a bomb itself that will cause God to arrive on Earth, it may be a near threat because the bombings might not stop at one only. But I remember God saying that an EMF bomb that would terminate all access to any power, and this could be it. This is why he wants us to prepare with food storage and sources of heat for a few months until they can restore another free source of clean power. God also said that when this happens nothing will work, not even weapons, they can do this. We can only wait and see.*

*These are really good questions Mike. What province or state are you from? I will publish these answers to your questions without your name because other people may have similar questions.*

*Be one with God. Amazing grace.*

*Johanne*

I thanked her in a response and told her that my wife and I were in the process of moving to another city that would be closer to our family and didn't know when I might present more questions. She told me I was welcome and that she *"found it difficult to say anything about this, questions really help.*" I felt pleased at that point of being able to help her and us at the same time. I was starting to imagine that she had been feeling somewhat isolated since revealing this information.

# Chapter 7
# Our Faith Background

Both Nana and I had been raised in the Catholic Faith. Her family was from a long line of French Canadian, German and Irish pioneers. After about 300 years in the Montreal area, the French families started the move southward. After a short stop in Connecticut, working in the logging business, they proceeded west to the Dakotas, and homesteaded there in the early 1870's. All had large families and they quickly adapted to the prairie life as farmers. The German ancestors all landed in the Eastern Iowa region near the Mississippi river and eventually made their way to northwestern Iowa. Both sides were Catholic through many generations. In a tragic turn of events, Nana's parents died in a traffic accident when Nana was only seven years old, leaving her and her brothers to be raised by her father's parents. They attended mass regularly, attended catechism classes as youngsters and were all married in the Catholic Church. One by one, the three all divorced their first spouses. Nana held on the longest as she wanted to make sure her children were born and raised in a home with both parents. She put her feelings away and suffered through a somewhat abusive relationship until that ended by divorce after 25 years and the children were now mostly grown.

I was born and baptized in the Catholic faith. My father was from a long line of many generations of German and Irish Catholics on both of his parents' sides, however; my mother was converted to the Catholic faith just prior to marrying my father. Her side was mostly Methodist, with a few Lutheran connections. She sometimes seemed to me to be the more "religious" of my two parents. In my father's later years, I discovered his deeply religious side, his daily prayer routine and his personal Bible, all things I saw his mother and his grandmother do also. They all did the same things in the end. I was the oldest of a large family. We attended mass every Sunday throughout my childhood. We also participated in Catechism classes, later renamed CCD classes. At one time, in about the 8th grade, we were studying as a class about religious orders and (how to become a priest or sister/nun). Another young man and I were chosen to be new priests in a mock ordination ceremony to show the class how this happens. I was always proud of that and proclaimed on occasion that I had been a priest at one time! As I grew up and was eventually on my own, my "routine" faith started to waver slightly and missing church on Sunday became more frequent. I found Sunday mornings to be a great time to go hunting or fishing, as there were not as many to compete with, as a large share were probably in church at that time. I had not lost my faith or my beliefs but the routine masses seemed like not much fun or were no longer informative. When I was going to marry, I had to reintroduce myself to the system. My future wife's family was also Catholic and that had been a desire of mine, to find and marry a woman of the same denomination as me. We attended the required marriage classes that were meant to make sure we were on the right path and in line with the teachings of our faith. They also tested our resolve and made sure this wasn't only one of the couple's idea, but both were committing. As planned, we married in the Catholic church. Some years we waivered a bit in attending mass weekly. As children came along, we tried to be good parents, we baptized them there and tried to do a better job of attending weekly services. We really did want them to acquire a good faith and belief system of their own. One day, after 15 years of marriage, I found myself in a divorce and soon I was a single man again, but this time I had two children to raise as their mother had stepped out of their lives. I decided I needed to be a better, faith filled man and do the right thing. We made sure our weekly and other church requirements were met and I tried to be on a better path of love for God as an example for my children to follow.  My children thought I had gone "overboard" when every Sunday morning I marched them down to the front pew or at least one of the first three so that, as I told them, they would be able to see what was going on better!  They resisted every week but followed my direction.  Our faith was increased and tested the next few years. Those things are written about elsewhere in this book.

After a few years had passed, I started dating again. Eventually, I found another who was also raised in the Catholic faith.  Prior to that, I had begun the only acceptable practice of making myself eligible to remarry, by going through the required Marriage Annulment process of the Catholic faith.  My now future wife, was never previously married so it was just a matter of my going through a fairly difficult process. They basically had to decide that there wasn't the commitment necessary in the beginning to warrant a binding event. In the church's opinion, it was not a marriage from the start.  A few weeks passed and a decision was made to dissolve the first marriage, making me free to marry again in the Catholic church. My second wife and I started a life together with my daughter from my previous marriage in tow.

I was so excited to be back on the path of a family man and we began trying to restart our dreams. Both of us felt some of life had passed us by and we committed to doing several things together in our quest for a happy and fulfilled home life.  Having children was one plan and living in the country another.  We started going to church together with my teenage daughter from the previous marriage.  I was happy about that but things changed rather quickly.  My new wife had started a new café in her hometown before we married and it was a 7 day a week job for her.  She started missing Sunday mass with me.  After a discussion about this, she agreed to stay home on Sundays and then we could go to church together.  After about a year and a half, our new daughter came into the world and we started going to church as a family.  I don't remember how long that lasted but eventually church goers saw only me and the tiny baby every Sunday by ourselves.  By the time she was 3, mom and dad had split and divorce number two became real for me.   One thing that remained consistent, was that now I never missed church on Sunday.  I had my tiny daughter most every weekend from the time she was 2 until she graduated from high school.  We attended mass every Sunday and she attended the preschool at our church as she grew.  There came a time she didn't go to mass with me and I started being there by myself.  I remember thinking once that through all of this time of my life, it has gone from my whole family involved in the Catholic faith, to now just me. Even my siblings had all strayed away to something different or nothing at all.  I resigned myself to just trying to be a good, faith filled man; to pray, to do things in good ways and to be a good

Catholic.    Over a lifetime of attending church, the Gospels all were very well known by me and as they were read over and over, year after year, decade upon decade, nothing changed.  The story was the same.  It was the same story on the same week, every year.  The only difference was the rotation of the four gospels written by Matthew, Mark, Luke and John, done on a four-year cycle.   Each getting their variation read during the sermons on their year.

Ten years more passed by and by chance, I met another.  She was kind, caring, good with children as she had been a teacher for decades.  She had a gentle soul.  A faith filled woman with a rural and small-town background such as mine.  She also attended the same church. I was so happy we had met.  I married Nana in 2013 in a private ceremony at our local parish with only our children, their spouses and grandchildren in attendance.  Prior to this event, I had helped the both of us go through the Annulment process once again for me and the first time for her.  We became a good Catholic couple, attended church regularly and occasionally a week day mass.  We talked about doing that more frequently.  I felt like I was back on track again and maybe I could be more in for my church. We purchased a home together that was only about 2 blocks from our church and I remember joking with the local priest about how I might be able to make it down there more often because we were within walking distance now!  I was also aware that our grown children were now all finding new churches to attend, with many new and more modern gatherings, unlike the old, ritualistic Catholic versions I grew up with. The last holdout was my oldest daughter, who got all of her three children through at least first communion age before leaving the Catholic faith for another denomination. I was sad to see that happen and I knew it was the end of things that I had such great respect for, because of tradition and loyalty. The grandchildren that now have come along, began being committed to their family's religious practices by a ceremony called being, "dedicated" and not being baptized anymore as babies. The Catholic practice was "Baptism" and eventually, "Confirmation" when a child grew to young adulthood. Both are "sacraments" in the Catholic faith. In these new church celebrations, "Dedication" is the family committing the child to the religious life of this church and later a "Baptism" when they become of age. Same things, different words. Anything to get the younger generation involved, including music selections during the services. The more ritualistic churches, old-time hymns are standard and in the new, modern religions, it's Christian rock. Even though I am an old "rocker," it is a little too loud in my opinion!

# Chapter 8
# I Need to Know More

My wife and I were so busy preparing for our move and yet, in the evenings, I was still very much active in my research into the book and related items found elsewhere on the internet. We talked about all of this frequently in our home. We did not attempt to say much about it to family or friends. Sometimes might drop hints or say things hoping to get a feel for how someone might react. Much to our chagrin, we never really got much traction telling others, so it became our "little secret." There did come a time that one more extended family member got interested and we remained connected to that person. We would read blog posts to her and give our opinions and discuss our beliefs. It was a relief to have another to talk to about this. We were not troubled by it, more so were hoping to help others understand. We found it almost impossible to inject this into the current reality that people were living in.

These messages in her book made me think about other things that needed clarification:

*"My scribe asked me today if I am the "Most High." Here is my answer to this question. I am God, I am the one who created Earth with the help of others and Sophia. She designed the renewal of social structure of all people. She created order and responsibility of choice and with her help we created a similarity to our evolution to open to our reunion time."*

(J. Howard, <u>The Wisdom of God,</u> 2020, p134)

*"I am knowing about the pain and sorrows of responses to war as I myself served under many commanders who knew only how to murder. They are as they wish to be and nothing can change them because they only see decreasing populations as a way to be victorious. This is a lust for power at the deepest psychopathy.*

*I was younger then. I helped in many places in the Universes as a mercenary who knew more than most, and as the stories of Ulysses, I traveled the universes with many troops to settle with the dark ones. Be certain my understandings are very clear about wars. And after thousands of Earth years, we arrive to Earth where I created life for a better answer to living in peace."*

(J. Howard, <u>The Wisdom of God,</u> 2020, p272,273)

On the 29th of April, 2021 I decided to write to Johanne again.

*Hello Johanne,*

*I have a few more questions and lots of curiosity. God obviously, knows about me but, I would like to know more about God.*

*I have a hard question to ask and not sure what would be accomplished by it but, As a "being" and our creator, how did God's existence come to be, as he clearly has stated he was, at one time, younger (fighting under commanders) and when asked about the "Ancients", he said he would be like them someday, a very long time from now, which describes an aging process, even if it is just a time of gaining more knowledge.*

*Next, did God create this whole solar system including the sun and planets or just Earth? Has he created other planets?*

*We have 4 distinct races of humans on Earth. Was that the original design at creation or has this been the result of an evolution or change in the human form over time, based on the early existence of humans in different regions around the globe and environmental effects on the body.*

*Has God ever created life forms elsewhere or is Earth the only place?*

*Thank you for your time again.*

*Mike Maher*

Those were a sort of an odd group of questions that were "outside the box" type and was my effort to start expanding beyond "known" facts I had accumulated over my time. Johanne answered some of these questions but not all on her blog and messaged me that she had done so.

*In this blog I wish to share questions I have received from a reader. Here is a summary of the questions, and following will be the response.*
*Questions:*
*How did God's existence come to be?*
*According to the information given in the book, God when younger served and fought under commanders. Is there an aging process? Is this to gain knowledge?*
*Did God create the whole solar system including the sun and the planets, or just Earth?*
*Has God created other planets?*

*Are we the results of evolution or change in the human form over time and/ or by environmental factors?*
*Has God created life forms other than on Earth?*
*Here are the responses through the message from April 30, 2021:*
*Be understanding these questions as asked are serving the key to who we are and what lives outside of Earth. This answers the better renewed truth that steps out of these lies told on Earth about us. These lies only serve those who have enslaved our children and are serving my children a great deception that only causes people to use each other without any care or respect (relating to the theory of evolution).*

*Presently, before we arrive, death is the only way to better understand what exists outside Earth. (Described in "The Egyptian book of the dead" or "The Tibetan book of the dead", navigating through Bardo). Lucifer cannot hold on to a soul who is working on the understanding of what evil is and does, but he can renew with the 'pulling back' of a dark soul to reanimate a body. Be this said, you cannot leave Earth ever unless you know how to navigate the dealers of lies who sell these ideas of eternal life only after you settle with them (the demons) by serving their lies and slavery.*

*God does not lie. So here are serving ways to answer these questions. First, we are living beings who are certainly living much longer than humans only because we are not on Earth. The atmosphere on Earth causes an early death that does not serve anyone other than Lucifer, who deals only in abuse to cause a person or animal to be dead and reincarnate the soul to answer to what the devil wants. And soon you will see for yourself how these ways are done in evidence of the stealing of souls.*

*Now Lucifer wants to cull humans to take these souls with him as he believes he will deal with his troops to leave Earth as we arrive. But this will only cause his own death and dealings of lies to be ended.*

*Know now this about serving these truths. You see these words about my Za's writings and better understand that only Earth is believed to be dealing with these troubles, but try to open to and share knowledge with others because soon they are coming to Earth to open to serving greater truth, and consequently seeing to better changes, and seeing this is healing death thinking.*

*God lives on a ship presently because more truth needs to be shared before these answers open to all people of Earth.*

*Secondly, these servants of Lucifer have been reincarnated many times to answer to better serving Lucifer. Evidence of this we know about because we are seeing this and seeing the settling of souls. The settling of souls means after death destiny serving with the same being and serving with another body, either through birth or body takeover you call possession.*

*And this is the problem about what evolution is theorized to be. These theories are meant to distract all humans from the truth and causes your mind to stop thinking and finding truth. And children are indoctrinated in home and in school education to stop imagining what could have really happened.*

*Now be unbelieving evidence of believed lies, and free your thoughts of these imposed constructs of what all is, and renew with answers coming from many others above Earth who have much to share with their spiritual families.*

*God sees all because these ways our Ancient ones taught us, and this means we are as humans are, but free from slavery and the settling questions to "why are we here?" These questions have answers and we are opening the way now for all people of Earth as we remove the darkness that has controlled Earth for so long.*

*Be dealing with these truth as you can but heal yourselves from all lies imprinted on your minds and open your heart to greater truth. Now answer this and be certain all starts as I said and understand these questions asked are very easy to answer and deal with because seeing is believing, and soon you will see who we are and understand how you were created and meet with your ijheer (spiritual) parents who wish to reunite with you and open to all truth.*

*This will be a glorious day and these days are very near. Soon all will be seen and all these lies served on you, will be dealt with and understood, and soon you will have all your questions answered in evidence of proof. This is a promise my children. Be renewing with all your families soon and renew with a greater life and truth of who you are.*

*And know these words are here more now because now all opens you to your story of past truths understanding all was never explained to you before. And the greatest sin on Earth started when Lucifer came and served a way of causing life to be shortened genetically and now, he is culling and selecting to take what he needs as he expects to be using these souls again.*
*But the truth comes and Lucifer will be removed and settling with his death only. This is the time now, proof comes soon. Question me face to face **Mike** because we have much to share together.*
*Now be ready.  God "*

This was my "come to Jesus" moment. Suddenly, God called me out by name.  I was, to say the least, "Shocked". The reason that I had been afraid to ask the questions that I mentioned in the beginning, had now become real.  This blog post had now become very significant in my path forward. Now it was highly personal.  If you could have seen the look in my wife's eyes when I read this to her, you would have seen the shock she experienced also.  Everything was changing rapidly as I let go of old beliefs and formed new.  My awakening was here.

In that same blog post, she added the following as she had asked for clarification.

*So this morning I asked for clarifications about Lucifer 'pulling back souls' and what that means. Here is the response.*

*Question: What do you mean by 'pulling back souls'?*

*Response: " ... many ask why does truth heal only with the death questions. Understand that this heals these questions because this serves all who settle with our knowledge only and heals those who return home. But 'pulling back souls' does more to stop those who do not belong with us and then evidence of seeing opens. Be renewing only with this knowledge now as much needs to be understood. And also, those who are renewing with us will answer to all their acts on Earth and this causes the pulling back of souls by Lucifer who does not want to let his beings of darkness be judged by us.*

*And pulling back that causes these souls to be better serving darkness are soon opening to being darker and causing more trouble for my children. My children also are pulled back and they settle with more troubled lives to experience* with many more attacks on them.*

*Be understanding these acts of darkness growing on Earth are multiplied by this and only serves with us. Because the evidence of the sorting of souls is well seen by many more people, this will help answers that will be shared in serving truth. These times as said are here now. All is soon now. God "*

(J. Howard, <u>The Wisdom of God</u>, Blog post April 30, 2021)

# Chapter 9
# Bodhi

The information I was getting was all making sense.  I was excited about digging deeper into many of the new understandings.  After the last series of emails, I had been doing some research and the result ended up in the next correspondence.  I emailed Johanne on May 12, 2021 and wrote these things:

*Hello again, Johanne,*

*Hope you are doing well.  I had a couple things I wanted to tell you about and comments on others…..*

*I reread the last messages that you gave me via your communications with God.  I broke each paragraph down and reviewed it and made my own interpretations. In general, I felt I was getting a "just wait and see" to my queries. That's okay but now it has stymied me a bit as I wonder, why ask any more questions? But, don't worry, I probably have a few more….. 😊*

*As I was reviewing those statements, one strange thing happened when I was doing a bit of side research on the mention you made of the Egyptian and Tibetan books of the dead, and navigating through Bardo. As I was reading that, the term, **Bodhi**, came up. I immediately texted my youngest daughter and asked her how she picked the name for her new dog, Bodhi. She said she just saw it someplace and thought that would be a good name and she asked why. I told her it was related to an awakening or an enlightenment period and she replied, "cool!" I didn't go further with that conversation but, thought that name selection and what I just found out, was a very strange coincident.*

*Do you still communicate via chart and pendulum? I'm curious as to why that would be the preferred way when we have so many other ways and they have telepathy?*

*Just yesterday, I was thinking about words that you wrote about God fearing that in the beginning of their descent onto the Earth, that people would be scared and not believing what they would be seeing and witnessing. Then I wondered if the emotion of fear is a barrier to understanding. That led to a thought, could the fear emotion, be a built in "cloaking" mechanism to hide evil in ourselves? I know it's a strange question but I would think God and his accompanying beings would be able to easily overcome the fear and anxiety of such a spectacle unless there is something else that keeps us from believing what we are seeing. That was just a random thought and I don't expect much of it.*

*I have to tell you that every night, when I go to bed, I pray to God and actually call him **God Yahweh**, as he called himself once in your writings. I pray only, for understanding. I have long prayed for wisdom. I am not fearing anything, not wanting anything materially, I have good health and a good family, I am retired and do whatever I want to, every day. I don't worry about money, or the future. I **do** worry about the evil influences that get stronger every day. I try to get news.......real news, by following as many people that seem to be on the right track, as I can. Your book, your blog and your messages are some of the strongest news I get. Your recent message from God, which stated that he and I will meet face to face as we have "much to share together" really has me baffled as I don't feel like I have much to share and seems that it would be more of a one-sided conversation!*

*I am always happy to see a new posting from you on the website and always hope to gain more knowledge or understanding with each. I am glad that you have spaced your messages out so they aren't an everyday thing, as that can lead to people not paying attention due to the routine but, I can assure you, they all mean something to me and probably everyone else that has read your book. Thank you for bringing us these messages.*

*Have a good day,*

*Mike Maher*

Johanne replied the next day with this message to me:

*Hi Mike,*

*Are there coincidences? Or is God trying to call his children to enlightenment? 'Bodhi' is a very interesting word as you are unraveling this knowledge.*

*I use the pendulum every day to connect with God, to me it is prayer (about 1:30 hours), and it is to confirm telepathy. I almost hear but I don't; the words come and I support them with the spelling of the pendulum because my mind drifts and my own thoughts interfere with the message. Years ago trying to understand myself, I searched for information on this telekinetic ability and found Prof. Valerie Hunt UCLA who wrote books on her experiments measuring auric fields. She used an instrument that measured energy/vibrations coming from healers as they were healing, and she found this energy to come from the body of the healer. And Dr R Hawkin, his book: 'Power vs Force' describing muscle-testing kinesiology to measure emotions strength. For example, he calibrated 18 emotions, a map of consciousness and here are some: shame=20, guilt=30, apathy=50, grief=75 ....... love=500, joy=540, peace=600, enlightenment=700, God=1000. (I made a chart of this map but I no longer use it). And also much research has been developed with the Montreal Cardiologie Institute engineers who were able to measure the distance of the heart's energy field, 8 meters but the instrument was limited at 8 meters. So, the heart and telepathy can reach very far. I am sure there is much more research on this but for me, it made me understand that we can be more than we are.*

*God engages in conversation mostly unless he wants me to listen and he says; "Now listen" and tells me what is important. We speak every day now but, in the past, also I spoke with Gabriel. He is comfortable with languages and current expressions; he explains things well. My experience with them was like deprogramming and instruction, in a loving way. They feel like family to me now but not at the beginning 18 years ago. It took me a long time to trust them, to believe who they are and why me. So, Mike, you can converse with God when you meet him face to face, it could be soon as he is arriving in person, this is what he tells me more than enough times.*

*When you described yourself, it sounded like me, I share the same feelings and I am retired. I am focusing on the change coming with God. He said in 2016 that the signs will be asteroids and meteors, and the war with Israel and Iran, and (I think) Hamas is funded by*

*Iran. I hope all is close, I am so looking forward to meeting them.*

*Anyway, I am not sure what to write in my blog this week. Something will come.*

*Take care, be with God, he is our Father of Heaven.*

*Johanne*

By this point in our connection, I was very happy that we had found Johanne, her book, her blog and developed a friendship though all of this.  Going from the dark days of the pandemic and the unknown future, to finding these revelations, was so uplifting.  Our spirits were happy!  Over the next couple of weeks, my wife and I moved to our new home and started the process of unpacking and putting our things away.  Happy to be nearer to our kids was such a boost to our morale, as we had been somewhat distant and not very accessible during the Covid days.  Life changed quickly for us as we became acclimated to our new surroundings.

# Chapter 10
# What is Heaven?

On June 13th, 2021, after a long talk with my wife, I wrote to Johanne again.

*Hi Johanne,*

*We have finally gotten moved into our new home, so now I have a bit more time to think about things in general. In discussions with my wife, the question about Heaven seems to be a focus of hers. She listens to what I tell her and what my understanding of what we have read in your book and then in later emails between us.*

*When we (anyone) talk about heaven, they look up or imply that heaven is "up there." The stars and solar system is "out there" in our universe. My wife has said many times that she wants to be in heaven. She wants to be with God. In many ways, that is the center of her beliefs. Our simple question, if it can be answered, is Heaven a "place," like a home planet or is it just the gathering of spirits in the presence of God, wherever he is?*

*I apologize for asking so many questions with long emails. Your answers help me understand what I feel has not been adequately explained in my prior education. I am searching for greater understanding and it seems to have pointed me to you. Following others to try to find truth that I couldn't find on mainstream news, led me to your video, which led me to your book, which led me to contacting you. What you have said and written, makes sense to me about a whole lot of things both political and spiritual.*

*It took a long time for me to write you the first time because I was afraid that some things I might ask would probably involve God answering personally. I don't have "contact" like you do and I fear being in that position myself, probably like you may have in the beginning of your contacts. But I have to ask things to get the answers, so I moved in that direction.*

*This morning, I watched the TV mass for our area, as I have for the last year and more. In mid-March of 2020, I attended the funeral of my grandfather's youngest cousin, who had died from a head injury suffered when he fell in his driveway. He was 91. That was the last mass I have attended and the last mass I received holy communion. That same week, our bishop announced that because of the pandemic, he was suspending masses until further notice. I am not a super "religious" person but of my 8 siblings, I am the only one that has continued the traditions of the Catholic faith. I can trace our Catholic heritage back to about 1800 in northern Germany and Poland. When we couldn't go to mass, my wife and I continued to watch it on TV every Sunday. With the discovery of your book, I have been trying to look at everything from a different viewpoint. I now think most everything is evil in its roots, but I know that some things must be good and under God's influence. It is so hard to know exactly what is right. So, I ask questions of you, that I might gain that ability to understand better and hopefully help others also.*

*I have known the torment of Lucifer that you have described. In the 1990s, I was immersed in torment and I struggled, but survived. My wife of 15 years at the time, left me for another. I discovered this as we were moving from Wisconsin back to South Dakota after three years living there. Only my two children made the move with me as my wife abandoned us. That being hard enough, soon my 12-year-old daughter was stricken with cancer. She survived and is now 41, married and has three children. When she finished her chemo rounds and was on the rebound, my son, my only son, was killed in a motorcycle accident. And there were other tragedies. With each I fell lower and lower. Things continued to happen, year after year, until nearly 20 years had passed. Then things got better, but now I felt old and worn out. I don't look for sympathy but I sure would like to find what caused these things and snuff it out of existence.*

*I don't remember my dreams much and if I do remember something, it is usually just a small part. Last night, I dreamt of my mother walking into wherever I was. What I saw was her at a younger age, maybe late 20's or so. She was as beautiful as I have ever seen her. She stopped and kissed me on the cheek and I just couldn't get over how young and beautiful she looked. She died 20 years ago from cancer. I rarely think of her but that was a welcome reminder of what I remember of her when I was a young boy.*

*Sorry for the rambling letter. I hope someday that I finally get the understanding I seek. Thank you for your help on this path I walk!*

*Mike Maher*

With this message, Johanne responded rather quickly and in a couple of hours she had this to say:

*Dear Mike and Mrs.,*

*Mike, please never apologize for sharing such important information with me. I am honored to hear your words and the path you are on. And I am very saddened by the loss of your son. Your dream is telling of what God said about people in Heaven being at the optimal age of 25-30 years old. It is so good that your mother reached out to you. And, I understand (from my own experiences) what made me ask God why we must suffer on Earth the pain of loss and betrayals.*

*Is your wife's name Anna? Could you share her name with me?*

*When I began receiving information from the spiritual world I also asked where is Heaven and what is Heaven. At the time I was answered that Heaven is a place, (many planets, the Pleiades), who live in peace and follow the Universal Laws. I was told that in Heaven people and animals live in harmony, there are plants, flowers and trees (large ones), and none are affected by any diseases, insects or reptiles. The wind and breeze from oceans are what helps pollination.*

*And about age, on Earth our DNA has been manipulated to age and die young to serve the purposes of the demons who enslave us. This also stops us from attaining our true mission, to reconnect with God. In the book of Enoch, people were described living for hundreds of years. Now we are seeing lives being shortened purposely with the true intent of the vaccines. (The local first nation people in North Vancouver have printed on many fences that the 'vaccine is a depopulation campaign'). Scientists say that we have 'junk DNA' that is useless. I think we are capable of telepathy and much more with this unused DNA. Healing this happens in Heaven. It might be more physical than we can imagine.*

*I had a dream about my mother after her passing. She lived in a beautiful place, she was young and peaceful, and from a large window I saw a sky with colors of gold, amber, pinks and purples. I think that was Heaven.*

*So this morning I asked God to describe Heaven to me again for your wife. Gabriel answered me saying that God was busy with others and that he could answer me. This I will put in my blog later today; it is quite interesting. We have been told by religions and clergy things that they themselves don't know. People who have near death experiences have much more to say about their soul reaching these other places. And it is often describing what God and the Archangels say.*

*Keep in touch, be well and may God watch over both of you.*

*Johanne*

When the next day came and Johanne posted her answer from Gabriel, we were very excited to read what he had to say. This was the first time we got to hear from Gabriel.

*" This is Gabriel. I answer you today, God visits with many. You are asking me questions that I will answer you now, and opens many to evidence of knowledge of who we are. We Archangels are living in the group of planets of the Pleiades because we are serving with many others who are serving with the Universal Laws, renewing all who are with us and opening to greater truth than seen by Earth beings. Now the Pleiades are more than our home, healing ways are serving many here, and many are answering with us renewing with the ways of our truth. Be understanding they settle with the thinking of usury and certain methods of enslavement through force, and they learn about cooperation and independent thought. So many see us as divine beings who honor the truth above all seen action, and better serving these laws that open to greater answers than seen on Earth. At the time of meeting, many will travel to these serving planets to learn about how all is and how all heals because we are dealing with the way believed to be understood truth, these answers are serving all. The non-believers are deceptive and have many dark plans that do not open to others but themselves. They believe they can act as they wish and they practice: "Do as thy will is the whole of the law". These ones are the ones you must free yourself from. Dealing with these ones will never serve you and soon beliefs are settling with them, as it is on Earth.*

*The questions asked are more than I can say, but I want to share this with you. My testament of Heaven is a place that has many houses and many kingdoms that*

> *live with the knowledge of perpetual peace and care and love for all life that wishes this. These stories you are told as children are true for a child, but only more than this as better seeing of this question opens to a time to be renewing with the view of an adult who understands the way God serves all knowledge to better all people and greater seen life. And understanding these words will help you see that our time to share knowledge on Earth heals many beliefs of who we are. Beliefs are only the truth unseen proof of what exists outside Earth.*
> *Be seeing this as truth and be one with us".*
> *Gabriel*

(J. Howard, <u>The Wisdom of God</u>, Blog *Is Heaven a Place?* June 14, 2021)


As mentioned in her last email prior to this blog post, she asked the question, "is your wife's name Anna? And could I tell her the name?" We talked about that, trying to figure it out and realized her middle name was Ann. But later I reasoned that maybe he meant, "Nana" as she was routinely called by the little ones and some of us adults! I asked Johanne, why the question, and she replied that in parts of the conversation not included in his message, Gabriel knew exactly who he was talking about and said her name was Anna. It is a mystery and a fun fact that it happened. On the 15th, I wrote Johanne and provided this information to discuss:

Johanne,

*I was happy to see the reference to the Pleiades planets (in your last blog) as I have seen them referred to on an episode of a Television show called, Ancient Aliens as the most likely home planets to beings referred to as the blue "light beings." These beings were described as having been involved in a large fight or war, with reptilian type beings, who were the victors. There is a mound the shape of a serpent in OHIO (if I remember correctly), that is supposed to be part of a monument depicting that war like event. That same show talked about the planets in that grouping also called the 7 sisters.*

*I did some searching on line today about the Pleiades and ended up in a group of search results where there are a large number of people who claim to be able to speak with the language of light or of the light beings. They claim to be able to converse with their hearts rather than their minds. I listened to some of the speech on videos and did not get anything from it. It seemed just like any other foreign language to me that I probably had never listened to. They called it "Saren," and I wondered if you had experience with this? I used your book and looked up some of the words you had written and did not find any that matched anything they had. The one lady said she used a chart and pendulum to get these words from the light beings. (similar to your method). I decided to leave that alone and quit researching it as it seemed to be more of a Wiccan type gathering spot, by the type of responses to the videos.*

*I have noticed an uptick in news stores trying to downplay the UFO reports that the US government is supposed to release soon. These are things they have kept top secret for 70 years or more, but are now releasing info. My guess is they are planning to get this info out, then persuade us that these probably are aliens and that they can't be good and we should not trust them. Much like what God worried about (in your book) that when they arrive, we would fear them.*

*Mike M*

Johanne was interested in what I said here, as there was commonality in her methods and those that I spoke of here. She responded with this the same day:

*Mike,*

*Where did you find this information about the lady using a chart and pendulum, and the language?*

*Honestly, when I started to get this information decades ago, I thought the messages were strange because I did not believe in Aliens, UFOs, or contacting "spirits". If anyone would tell me they talked to God or Angels, I would try to avoid them thinking they had a mental illness. I thought what I was doing was my imagination or maybe a gov. MK ultra type experiment but there is much more to this than I can put together. (It took years before I was deprogrammed). I think in the book, God speaks about the Gersils, anyway in my conversations he has. I never heard about the Gersils before and I thought I made it up (sounds like gerbils, my son had gerbils). But recently I heard a man from the ECETI Ranch say the word 'Gersiels', and he said they would arrive first and soon. I was surprised. ECETI is a place near Mt Shasta where people see UFOs.*

*Thank you for looking into this, I am really interested, I have lived as a solo hermit for too long.*

*Keep me informed please.*

Every correspondence between us was bringing more and more information and I felt we were gaining so much knowledge, sharing with Johanne. For the next few months, we would email often back and forth about a variety of subject matter. We both were searching for answers, and with two of us looking in many different directions, we kept putting more little pieces of the puzzle into view. Sometimes they fit and sometimes not.

# Chapter 11
# Beings

In the previous couple of emails, we were talking about "alien" races and far off planetary systems. All are part of this story. The Gersiels, for example, have been identified as the race that will start cleaning the waters of Earth, once they have come. In the book, God says the Nordics will come first as part of the repairing of Earth. He also mentions the "greys" and the reptilians at other times. He also identifies Lucifer as a reptilian in one statement. It does not take much to go on the internet and look up alien races and descriptions. Fantasy or real? Most people understand the information that has been presented through time about strange space craft or alien beings that get reported. Many times, they are ridiculed or not believed. However, lately, the US Government hearings have produced more unexplained things. Claims have now been made public in those hearings of finding dead and living "Biologics" in crashed UAPs. Biologics are beings.

Some of the beings God mentioned in the book and their purposes are:

> *"We call them another name better suited for them but they call themselves the "Gersiels." They arrive with us and serve to be the healers of the waters of Earth. The beings who are with us are mostly humanoids however only some are coming with us as not all are serving on our missions, nevertheless they all accept the ways of the Universal Laws. Tell yourselves that many exciting times awaits you as you will renew with many others."*

(J. Howard, *The Wisdom of God,* 2020, p168)

> *"These ones are called the "Nordics." They will come first to answer to the moving out of all governments from all Capital Cities. And then, we will arrive to settle into positions of law, and answer to all injustices according to the ten commandments and the laws dealing with the Universal Laws. These Laws are more than any other, and deal with the truth and not tricks to take from the innocent."*

(J. Howard, *The Wisdom of God,* 2020, p213)

# Alien God

In <u>The Wisdom of God</u>, Johanne wrote many entries of God speaking about their ships. He also spoke of the time of reunification when they come, that they will be accompanied by many from the many universes. Some will look similar to us and some may be very different looking. God was answering questions in 2012 and had this to say about some of the beings:

*"Now about the questions from Canada and the USA about how we arrived because the sightings of our ships are not yet seen. We have not all arrived. Some scout ships as said have become seen by the serving cameras, but we the Elohim have not arrived yet. We are the ones you see but the ones who are on Earth are from the Pleiadean planets, as you call them.*

*Be certain they serve with us and are serving to answer you as they prepare all information to be well shared by all who are ready to land. The Pleiadeans are mostly like humans but they are not all as humans. The seeing of some may appear difficult to look at, but we do not see them this way anymore as they are kind and caring to all of nature, animals and humans.*

*Be certain they are soon coming also to walk the Earth with us. The seeing of these humanoids may frighten some of you but be serving respect to their beliefs and goodness, and they are grateful and serving to all. Be ready to be answered by them as they have much knowledge about repair to pollution damage and they are well prepared to clean the oceans and water ways.*

*Be dealing with these good souls as they are wanting to come with us to open to our ways of dealing with the cleaning of Earth."*

(J. Howard, <u>The Wisdom of God,</u> 2020, p168)

# Chapter 12
# Where do souls go now?

It was now February of 2022 and I had not asked any questions of much significance lately. I had recently lost people that had been in my life and had to find out what happens to those that pass, as the book seemed to explain, we are out of the "grasp" of the reincarnation cycle created by Lucifer.

"He created a loop with a magnetic field that returns all souls to him, to reinstall a programming that serves him. This programming called "Vishnu," the preserver, was designed by us when he came to our planet. Be understanding that this served his purpose of slavery well, as he began to use it on reincarnating souls who chose to come to earth, and they remained there (here.)

We answered to calls of prayers to be free again, but we could not return ourselves because a war was stopping us. Soon we start to unite and served these ways of Setu truth. And now all of us will arrive to free souls from perpetual reincarnation and abuses caused to stop the evolution of the soul. More than you are expecting answers you and deals with the truth of how all is healing with us."

(J. Howard, The Wisdom of God, 2020, p. 271)

On the 13th, I wrote these questions:

*Good Morning Johanne,*

*I had a thought this morning and I was wondering if you could answer a couple of questions.*

*Recently, several people I have known have passed away. Most from old age but some from cancer and some from covid as reported. Every time I mention a death to Nana, I say "Hmmm, I wonder if they were vaccinated?", knowing full well that they probably were. Anyway, my thought was, I wonder if Lucifer's reincarnation cycle is still operating and if these souls are still caught up in that. If not, where do the souls go? I had a few thoughts of them going to nearby ships in God's armada for healing, or do they get whisked away to some distant place for the same healing?*

*I know that recently in your blog post, you wrote that God said he was dismantling the grid that locks us in. If that is so, I thought the souls could finally get out to be healed.*

*If we are here now, have we been in this cycle of reincarnation? Have we lived here for several lifetimes? Or, have we chosen this time to be here on Earth to help with this end time situation?*

I also had mentioned we were having a winter storm and cold spell and I worried a bit about a power outage possibility.

Johanne wrote back a couple of hours later and had this to answer me:

*Mike,*

*A few things, first (more friend advice) get a generator and fuel to keep warm, and second, more supplies. These are the times of preparations God told us about.*

*Okay, the big answers.*

*"Yes I know about Mike's ponders, but I will tell him only this, trust that all will become well settled. Understand how answers are settling with the way of greater responses, and be certain how all truth will be shared in a short time. More will be understood about*

*the visits settling with us as that nears, and more will be dealing with greater seeings in a short time".*

*(Mike you just got the 'sit on your laurels' answer, but I pressed on politely about the other questions).*

*" Lucifer has a hold on many souls as we speak: dead, as you think death is, and alive through possession of souls in humans, but these alive souls are willingly serving with this monster. Many have renewed their commitment to serve Lucifer after another life and more. Those who are trapped and do not respond to lives of abuse to serve Lucifer are calling on me to free them, and this I know, and this I want to better explain. They ask to be free from the works of evil, and they ask to be free from the seeing of greater lies. But I cannot open this yet because we are at war with the entities outside Earth. And the battle that settles with this will end this responding prison in evidence of what is now healing on Earth with my children's cries for freedom.*

*Understand Mike, you will be seeing all as it is now unraveling and you will be determined to answer to Me directly, as my Za has seen as better to onm (share information) with us, but this heals your heart only. So be ready for My words to come to you soon face to face. Be seeing the evidence of the Holy Spirit who answers to many who ask why, and be understanding how many trusted truths open to better times. And be renewed by the coming days because all will be renewed soon with us and become greater truths soon".*

*Hum. This is the last great battle for the freedom of God's children. Do you mind if I publish this answer to you?*

*Blessings, and stay safe.*

*Johanne*

So, here again, I am answered by name and was feeling that I was irritating him slightly. As I read it, he was saying you will get your answers and please be patient. He almost seemed like he thought I was pushing towards getting direct contact and he was explaining that it would not do me any good because it would only heal my heart, make only me feel better. Truth be told, I would not mind it, but it may be a greater responsibility than what I probably realize. He mentioned the name "ZA" here again and that is what they call Johanne. She has told me that he has used her given name before in communications, but this is what she is usually called and is explained in her book. She is described in the book as a "scribe" and God states this in the book a few times.

# Chapter 13
# Johanne's Story

From the cover of **The Wisdom of God,** 2020:

*Johanne Howard was born in Quebec and educated in French Catholic schools. She completed a college degree in Theology, a university degree in Social Psychology of Communication, and later moved to British Columbia to further her studies in education. She is a French high school language specialist who works and lives in North Vancouver, British Columbia with her husband, her two sons, two dogs and two cats. She has an enduring curiosity and a developed interest in the study of religions, esoteric knowledge, spirituality, and especially a constant search for the truth.*

On April 29, 2022, I emailed Johanne with some of my thoughts about current events:

*Hi Johanne,*

*How are you doing? We are well and fine. The women of the family have a baby shower in Omaha tomorrow, for my youngest daughter, who is due in June. It's about a 3-hour drive from here so they all will be gone most of the day. I'll just stay home and cook something* 😊

*I am writing to tell you I just completed reading your book again for the 3<sup>rd</sup> time! It actually seemed easier this time. I guess I am getting used to the repeated phrases. I took really good notes this time and when I got done, I had more questions than answers. Don't worry, I don't have any plans to ask for many more answers. It's all gotten so overwhelming to me. Life was simpler before I decided to "dig deeper." It gets frustrating, knowing things that I cannot do anything about such as sharing with family or friends. Nana and I talk about everything but even she has gotten to the point that she just wants to see something happen…..anything to show progress out of the stuff we have all been dealing with the last 2 years. I know that we've really had it easy, as I see what others have had to face.*

*It's raining and just started to thunder and some flashes of lightening so I better get off this computer!*

*Take care,*

*Mike Maher*

She replied to this email on the next day, April 30th. We had both been trying to figure out what was the status of how things were progressing towards what we believe is the entrance of God and his heavenly army, led by Jesus and Gabriel. If it hadn't been noticed before in these exchanges, Johanne is in Canada. Her viewpoint of Government and life there is slightly different from mine, here in the US.

*Hi Mike,*

*How am I? I am in awe as I watch all unravel in the world. God said he is allowing the division of souls to take place, and it is becoming so obvious, I'm speechless (or write-less). I'm watching the events in Ottawa now. The Veterans have arrived and so have crowds of people, including 800 police officers (employees of the Crown and WEF). When God says something is going to happen, it usually does, eventually. But also, things can change as humans have free will.*

*Here is a sad and difficult situation that our family has to endure. My sister's son, my nephew, disappeared about 10 years ago. He had 4 young children, now teenagers. His marriage was in ruins. We believe the disappearance had something to do with his wife and her boyfriend because he was previously threatened by the boyfriend. The police were useless; they did nothing and basically told us he probably did not want to be found. My sister resolved to stay near the grandchildren with concerns of the ex being abusive. God told us that the ex had cancer and would not survive, and one year later we found out she was diagnosed with cancer. Presently, the ex is in the last stages of cancer. God is also informing me that some people know about what happened to my nephew because the ex said something to people on a blog. But I cannot verify or do anything about it. My sister is very careful around her because she is verbally abusive and threatening. All in all, it is in God's hands and he knows this woman's destiny. It is so difficult to wait for justice and truth.*

*We are not all on the same path of knowledge, and the subject of a spiritual war is not clear to many. So, it is a lonely path and patience is needed. Faith, it seems at times too much to expect to have.*

*I am impressed that you have read the book three times. I would be happy to see your questions.*

*Be well my friend, and enjoy your cooking time.*

*Johanne*

I replied after a time of researching another suggestion she had of things to consider.  On May 1$^{st}$, I wrote the following to her:

*Johanne,*

*I am truly sorry that your family has been dealing with the loss of your nephew and the issues with his (ex?) wife. I have seen other long-term issues that have tormented family and or friends through the years and the only thing that was common to the end of those issues was that, as time passed, it slowly faded away. Time "heals" all wounds. To dwell on these things just eats a person up inside. I wish peace and closure to your sister and to you and the family.*

*I do believe we as humans, have spent way too much time "improving our intellect" and only side energy on improving our "spiritual" abilities. I do also have a belief that we are using only a small portion of our brain and in that, we can do things that are or should be, impossible, like psychic abilities. Just finely tuned concentration can do "magical" things. I studied a book once called, the "Zen of Archery". It taught me to "be the arrow." I was a semi-great competitive archer. I had gotten to a place where I could not improve my accuracy/ scores. Upon reading and understanding the message of the book, I was able to bring my focus to be a finely tuned instrument that guided the arrow to its mark. I became almost machine-like in my routine. Not in a superstitious way, but in my focus on consistency in form and process. I eventually won so many times, that one day, I lost my drive to be competitive and moved on; mostly because life events took away my reason to win. So, I think we have great capacity to do more with our brains than to just learn useless facts. Life is only so long for all of us, 70 to 90 years for the majority. We waste so much time doing things that really don't matter. Then, if like me, you waste even more time thinking about the time you've wasted! My opinion on these two subjects is, that yes, I think spirit and souls exist but I am not sure if we really can be in touch with them the way these ways promote.*

*That brings me to say this……..What is a soul anyway? Is it the same as a spirit? Is it a life form that needs a "vessel" like a body to live it so that it can improve its understanding of all things? Is it just a shapeless mass of energy? If it is life, why is life in a tree different than that in an animal? Or is it?? I am fascinated by the whole idea of reincarnation and the reasons of and for it as this seems central to the concept God had for humans. Lucifer also had ideas for the use of the cycle. I could see the value of creating a "vessel" like the human body design, then shapeless energy beings having the ability to inhabit it, to have experiences that they normally wouldn't have in their shapeless forms. That way, they could inhabit bodies of different life forms to experience all there is and someday know everything because they were able to gain those experiences. Think of it like driving a car. You get in it as the life form that makes it do things as long as you are in it. Then you get out and get into a different car and you make that one move and do things. The vessel doesn't remember all that happened but you (the life form) does and you take those memories with you. Okay, that's enough of that!*

*My book questions will start to follow soon. My initial questions will be about Sophia. So prepare yourself! (lol)*

*Thank you for listening to my rants.*

*Mike M*

On the 2<sup>nd</sup> of May, 2022, Johanne responded with this information:

*Hi Mike,*

*You are an Archer and were a competitive Archer. My sister takes her grandkids to an archery club. They all have their bows, and my sister also practices with a long sword. We were competitive equestrians. I used to train horses and teach. But I left that world when I moved to BC and my sister in Ontario still has her retired horse. How interesting! I tried archery when I was in my twenties with a friend who (sadly) hunted caribou with a bow.*

*Have you heard of Steiner schools and Waldorf schools?*

*Here is my story that opened the way for me to be contacted by God and the Angels. At UBC during my teacher education studies, we looked at different teaching philosophies. One of these was the Waldorf schools. It was briefly explained as an art school, a traditional German education and a spiritual education. At the time I was dissatisfied with the Catholic teachings and wanted to learn more. One day as I was driving not far from my home, I saw the school sign VWS Vancouver Waldorf School, and I heard (what I thought was my alter-ego) "you will teach here".*

*One week later, I saw an ad in the paper for a position for a French teacher; I applied, I was interviewed, and got the job. The internet and easy access to information was not yet a thing. I knew nothing at the time about this secret society, its background and aims. The first day of meetings as I walked through the doors, I heard my alter-ego voice say "this is a witch's den" and laughed at myself. Strange things happened there, and I started to read the books that were kept in a locked room. Esoteric stuff written mostly by Rudolf Steiner that was murky, unclear and I thought it was because it was poorly translated from German. And when I found the stuff about Lucifer, I thought it was a psychological metaphor. I had no idea it was a Luciferian cult. Verses were repeated before meetings and such, but I could never remember them and after ten years of working there I still needed to read the verses.*

*Yes, I worked there for ten years! I saw it the way I wanted to see it until I was able to access information from the internet and read and read, and then I wrote a poem to God and told him how my heart hurts. I started to ask questions at the school; my questions were not welcomed and then I was attacked in despicable ways based on lies and later fired.*

*Before I was fired, Uriel the Archangel answered me through the pendulum, he told me what the school was doing and it was time for more information. Uriel and Raphael guided me for a short time: Raphael was impatient and "grumpy" with me but he did help me with some health issues. And later after what seemed to be arguments/discussions among the Angels, Gabriel took over. He was a better English communicator and made more sense to me. (I was not very successful in learning/conversing in their language). He said they tried to reach me a long time ago but I was "lona" stubborn. Maybe a year after God began speaking to me, I was in complete disbelief still thinking I was suffering from a strange mental illness. God's English at the time was old English, not current but strong and authoritarian. I was never afraid. So, we began my reeducation starting with the Book of Proverbs. Every morning for a time, God would tell me to read a particular proverb and He would explain it to me. That very same day I would see the Proverb in action, it was stunning. Example: a person winked at me crossing my* path in the hallway at the school, she had ill-intent towards me as the proverb said that morning.

It was such a nightmare for me as this school tried to smear me and cause problems for me, I don't know how I could have survived this without God and his Angels. Typically, I blamed myself for everything wrong that could have happened. Their support saved me and showed me the truth.

By the way, all of the communications are recorded in hand written journals. In the beginning I spent 3 to 5 hours communicating every day. I learned about this cult and their plans to turn everyone to serve Lucifer. The UN library is dominated by books from Steiner, Blavatsky, Bassant, Crowley, Pike and other freemason type secret societies are all there. There are all these secret societies that are infiltrated in all areas of boards, foundations, politics (of course), medicine, social structures, religions, eugenics and much more. At the school, I helped with the moving of many new white boxes full of newly printed books from someone's personal garage to another hiding place and I was told these books were the blueprints of a new society.

I am so sorry this is long but somehow, I think it is important to share with you. These are amazing times.

God bless you Mike,

Warm regards to Nana.

*Johanne*

*PS. Recently, God talked about the soul and I was going to publish what he said, and because you asked, I will share this sometime this week when my mind is clear and focused.*


And so, it was now detailed out, how she first became contacted and where this story began.  I responded on May 5th with some comments and started more questions to discuss with her.  The email read in part:

# Chapter 14
# Questions about Sophia and Mary

*Good afternoon, Johanne,*

*Thanks for sharing your story about the beginning of your communication with God and the Angels. Your story is amazing, to say the least! The information about the demonic schools, institutions and governments goes with what I have been saying to Nana, that there is almost nothing that isn't touched by evil these days. Even things we believe to be good, maybe aren't.*

*Now I will start asking questions I have after reading your book again. You know, I am really just very curious about everything you have brought to us in the book and the blog messages. I appreciate all that you have already done to answer my queries.*

*Today I am going to ask about Sophia. I have asked you before but I couldn't find my emails with you on the subject. I am sure I have them but we have corresponded many times and I have a whole lot of them to go through to find specific things. I asked once about why there was no mention about "Mary" as mother of Jesus as we have been taught. God says in your book that Sophia is the mother of Jesus and the Archangels. Not knowing what kind of beings, we are dealing with here, and if a birthing process took place or just a term used for a motherly image or "position." In the book, God says something about Sophia being the one who visited the children at Fatima. In most of the apparitions that have been reported in history, they usually call the lady, the "holy mother" so a name isn't used and we just assume "Mary". I followed the apparitions of Medjugorje, every month for years. There were monthly videos of the crowds gathered to watch Mirjana Soldo experience the visions, which started in 1986 in Croatia.*

*God mentions Sophia twice in your book as the "second coming". Of course, much of what He says is outside of my ability to understand what He is talking about, but in a way, he isn't expecting us to understand, but to know, when the time comes. He says Sophia is incarnate and is on Earth currently. She kind of understands who she is, but wants to keep that to herself and continue to live a private, reflective life. She doesn't want humans to know who she is. I understand all of that but in the Bible, "Mary" never dies but ascended to "Heaven." There are conflicts in my understanding of who the Holy Mother is and what parts I struggle with connecting the truths.*

*In the, book God says to follow Sophia and Uriel. On page 16. I did a bit of research on Uriel. He is the Angel of Poetry also called the "Master of Knowledge." Has been called the Angel of Wisdom. Sophia means Wisdom.*

*So, my question is, do you think you could be Sophia? Uriel who is the Angel of Poetry, was the first to communicate with you. They call you Za. It can mean "my love" in some languages. I'm almost embarrassed to ask, but I thought I must. Please try to understand what brings me to this question. This is the hardest question I have to ask. More will come soon.*

*Wishing you a good day and evening,*

*Mike*


On the 8th Johanne replied:

*I published another blog just moments ago. My sister will go over it to check for errors, so I may have to fix it later.*

*To answer your questions about Mary and Sophia, it is on the blog. And to answer about me being Sophia, all I can say is I am a scribe, I know others are also receiving on Earth. I did not know that Za was more than a term of friendship. I am on Earth in life as you are. Anyway, I am with God no matter what or why.*

*I am fascinated by Mirjana Soldo from Medjugorje and her visions. I had a good friend who went there for a pilgrimage. She was a charismatic Catholic; she had a position in the parish church and she spoke in tongues with her group. What are your thoughts about people who speak in tongues?*

*Thank you for your inspirational questions, it helps me write.*

*God bless you and Nana.*

*Johanne*

*Messages from May 6, 2022; Sophia and Mary*

*My question here was on behalf of Mike about Mary and Sophia. Is Mary the reincarnation of the Sophia being?*

*He said: " Yes, she was my bride better suited to be the Mother in evidence of a doorway for the reincarnation of my son Jesus (Teacher). I wanted to reawaken her to share knowledge with Me and with Jesus, but she was not able to after the Christ's death and His return to Me. But she will awaken and serve her place by Me and the Archangels, and she will be with Teacher/Jesus the second coming. And these days are very soon and the time is now". Question: Did Mary become consecrated? He said: " She always was being the true Mother of all, and this heals as she awakens. And she will open to her time on Earth with us as we arrive and as Gabriel announces the truth to her".*

J. Howard, <u>The Wisdom of God</u>, Blog May 6, 2022)

I responded on May 9th, 2022:

*Hi Johanne,*

*Many thanks again, for your messages here and on the blog. I, and it seems, many, find strength and love in your messages from God.*

*Our family is well and thriving. Everyone is busy with life. We are just waiting now for my youngest to have her baby girl. She's due in a month. I was 44 when my daughter was born. I'm more the age of a grandfather to her and have told her that many times. She calls me "old man"* 😊

*Your answers about Sophia are much appreciated and I am satisfied with the clarity. I too, have had friends visit Medjugorje and I had planned on making a visit myself, with a friend from work. I actually delayed going a couple of times for different reasons. The one friend from my work has gone several times and got to spend time with Mirjana, in her home. He told me something that now has come back to make me question things there. He said, on display in her home is a pair of the Pope's shoes that he gifted her. So, another belief I had is now questioned.*

*Your question about my thoughts on people who speak in tongues.........If I had a protestant religious group upbringing, I probably would be more knowledgeable on the subject. Being raised Catholic, I never was exposed to anything like it. I would liken it to the recent videos I've watched about "light language" which supposedly channels "light being" communications. I cannot say one way or another, what good or evil it may be. That goes for almost everything I see anymore. It's kind of sad that this is how things have become for me. The questions I ask are all in the hope of finding direction.*

*With that, I have a few questions to ask after reading your book again. Please answer when you have time.*

- *On page 178, God spoke of the attack on Iran but said that you did not want to write about that (the attacks that were coming). Why not?*

- *Not much is ever said of the Archangel, Michael. I was raised thinking he was the main Archangel and the leader of God's army against Lucifer. Gabriel seems to be more involved in our human existence than Michael. Your thoughts on him?*

- *The last subject is the fallen Angels. My education was that there was a great heavenly war between God's Angels (led by Michael) and Lucifer (a fallen Angel), one who was once one of God's Angels. In your book, God says plainly that Lucifer is a Reptilian, not of God's group of beings. He was not an Angel. But several times in the book, God speaks of the fallen Angels. I get the feeling that the fallen Angels are ones that Lucifer convinced to join him and his methods. Just who are these beings that are named the fallen Angels?*

*I had a story I was going to tell you about a former coworker of mine who passed away a couple of days ago from Cancer. I decided it would get too long and maybe another time. This one guy caused the majority of my grief and destroyed all the good things I tried to do in my last decade of work. I didn't hate him but it was very close to hate. These bad feelings were greater than I have ever had for anyone else I have known. If I would have hated him, he would have defeated my ideas and my plans even more. I always treated him with respect and kindness and I think that was my strength to continue on. In the end, I had to retire as I didn't want to fight the fight anymore. I expect Lucifer would recycle his tormented, evil soul. His death has now caused me to think back to those days, when he made my life a living hell and all I get is empty feelings. Through all of my life's tragedies, things always end with an empty feeling. A battle won? I survived another attack on my soul. I look forward to the feeling I will get with God's triumph over evil!*

*Thank you for "listening" and thank God for blessing us with you!*

*Mike*

And so, we continued the discussion and she responded with this on the 10th of May:

*Hi Mike,*

*Always a pleasure to hear from you. I hope everything goes well for your daughter and the new baby.*

*Your questions are thought provoking. First, the question about p.178 in the book. If I remember correctly, the year I wrote this I was still struggling with messages/predictions that did not come to be. So, I was weary of sharing world events and personal things with an open blog, wanting to be responsible. What happens is that people plan things and then change these plans. At the time (2012), there were protests in Iran, missiles being tested, Obama making speeches, and large earthquakes killing many. But I cannot remember exactly what my reservations were about.*

*Micheal. He is a great leader serving God and His armies. He has a strong presence and has a big energetical vibration. He is friendly, warm and (a bit) formal. He communicated in the beginning (2003-2004). (I should dig out those books and reread ... ).*

*His story is when he battled with Lucifer, as Lucifer was losing, Lucifer said something to him that was deeply personal. This stopped Micheal from killing Lucifer. I am not sure if that is in the book.*

*Fallen Angels. The best rendition of the fallen Angels and how they came to be that way, is from Milton's book Paradise Lost. There you will find the names of the fallen ones and more. This is an amazing book for things that were not taught to most of us Catholics. I believe that the fallen Angels retained some abilities they had before like telekinesis and telepathy.*

*Your experience working with this now deceased man is difficult to hear. Your resolve to continue to be respectful and kind is outstanding. And now your feeling of emptiness around that experience seems to be the right response, you completed the experience.*

*Also, I understand your good discernment about "light language" and people who channel. Actually, I have little to no trust in these ways (including meditation) because how can I know who they are talking to, and I understand people who would say the same about my communications. I guess we will have to find out, all I can do is share and expect people to consider it themselves.*

*Until it is proven to be true, I observe all information, that means I listen and discern but trust very little, like I read you are doing. This is the path of wisdom.*

*Mike, be well and God bless you, Nana, your family and the soon to be seen little baby.*

*Johanne*

*PS. I edited the last 2 blogs.*

*PPS. Why did Mirjana accept these shoes from the pope? Was it meant as talismans or items of adoration?*

After receiving this message, I contacted my former workmate and asked the story behind the gift of Shoes. Then I let Johanne know.  The reply was this:

> *"The shoes at Mirjana's were given to her by Pope John Paul II.  He said that as pope he could not travel there unless invited by the presiding bishop (at the time the bishop was very anti-Medjugorje).  So, he gave her his shoes so that at least his shoes could be there."*

Johanne mentions that she wasn't sure the story of Michael and Lucifer was in the book and it was not.  I had noticed that she has had a few stories that she has referred to through the years that were very interesting, but did not make the book.

To this point, I have been trying to expand my field of view regarding all things related here.  The search for truth continued to widen.

# Chapter 15
# Archangel Azrael

As I was growing up, I was taught about Angels and Archangels. The Archangels seemed to be more powerful and the leaders. I really only knew (or remembered from my teachings) a couple of the Archangels by name. Gabriel, as the messenger of God and, Michael as the "General" and leader of God's army were the only two names I recalled. Through my discovery of these words I was being exposed to, I researched many subjects that came out of discussions with Johanne. Archangels was one of those. It started with her telling me about Uriel, the Archangel protecting Earth and Sophia. In a roundabout way, I present to the reader another Archangel, Azrael.

In a previous chapter I spoke of Bodhi, meaning a time of enlightenment. This is also described as the time in between; between life and death. After reading about this, I wrote to Johanne and told her a story of an event that happened many years prior. On July 15, 2023, I wrote:

*Johanne,*

*After sending you two emails, you would think that is all I have to say for a while. Instead, I must tell you something about Azrael. I think I have seen him before.*

*I did not know anything about this Archangel until today. After I sent you the first email, he showed up on two different lists from my Gematria searches and I decided to investigate. He is known as the Angel of Death; the Angel of transition from one existence to another.*

*About 50 years ago, I went hunting with my father, some brothers and friends. We had two vehicles and traveled 50 or more miles from my parents' home in the Black Hills of South Dakota, to the desolate prairies that exist to the north and east. These lands are like deserts. Barren land, rarely a tree in sight. We were either hunting for deer or antelope, I do not remember. What I do remember, is the trip home. When we decided to drive back home, I started out first and at some point, the other vehicle got about a half to ¾ mile behind me. (The land is mostly flat and you can see for miles) There was almost no traffic out there, so it wasn't hard for me to see them in my rear-view mirror.*

*As I got to the start of the mountains, I got to a section of highway that on one side is a small creek and on the other a sheer cliff of about 50 feet straight up. As I entered the curved road, I noticed a person sitting on the edge of the road on the cliff side. As I went by, I noticed him staring at me. He looked like a classic hobo or homeless man. He stared at me almost as if he was glaring at me. It spooked me then and I remember it still. We had 25 miles to go so it was an uneventful drive the rest of the way.*

*When our carload got to my parents' house, we waited for the others. After a long hour or so, they finally arrived. We asked what took them so long. They said they had to stop for the accident. Apparently, a 19-year-old had gotten between our vehicles somewhere along the last couple of miles and he lost control of his car and careened off the road to the right and into the creek, upside down and died there. My father and crew came upon it and said the wheels on his upside-down car were still spinning, but thought we had seen it because we were not that far ahead of them. I asked, "Did you see the hobo guy there?" and they said there was no one around. In that stretch of road, there is nowhere to go. It is sheer cliff on one side and the creek on the other. My theory was that the hobo, must have walked across the road and the kid swerved to avoid hitting him, lost control and died in the creek. But, in the time that passed between me driving through that area and my father coming along, was probably only a minute or two, not long enough for a pedestrian to go very far at all. So, from then on, I have always told people that I think I saw the Angel of Death and just today, all these years later, I now have his name,* Azrael.

*MM*

Johanne responded the next day with her email. I note here that I have toyed around with Gematria and had been sending her some of those results to consider, as another way we are being "informed" about how all connects. Gematria is the use of Numerology involving reading words and sentences as numbers and assigning numerical instead of phonetic values to each letter. Then you can compare those to other similar words/phrases with the same numeric value, much like using it as a decoder of sorts. I was finding words that had the same numeric value. For example, The Bible=Azrael and divine, and Bodhi = gold and death, using A=1, B=2, etc.

She had this to say:

*Hi Mike,*

*I read all your emails and I was going to bring to your attention Azrael, the archangel of death. I looked up a few sites and I wanted to send you one that had a reasonable description of his purpose. Death is not death; it is a transition. It reminds me of "The Tibetan Book of the Dead" or "The Egyptian Book of the Dead".*

*https://www.learnreligions.com/meet-archangel-azrael-124093*

*It's a fascinating description of events you experienced and now recognize. As well as, the gematria results that create meaning and repetition. It appears to be a method of communication that would reach your understanding. I would pay attention to it. In this morning's message: " Shared knowledge is coming from your seer Mike who responds to greater ways and who decodes our messages".*

That was a surprise answer and response and is one of the reasons I still sometimes do a search of words that seem to keep "popping up" some days. One day as an example, I kept seeing or hearing the word, "Lincoln." All day driving, reading, watching TV or whatever I was doing, it kept coming up. I researched it as I do whenever this happens. The resulting answers some times are very interesting and it almost reads like a headlines review of current events.  Things that make you go, hmmmm……..

I gave Johann a list of words as an example of all the same number value as "painting":

*Lastly, my desk faces the street.  Across the street they are painting the house north of us.*

*Gematria for <u>Painting</u>:*

*Hidden Codes; Antarctica, Boomerang, Matthew (the name God used for my son),*
*Polaris, the moon, Pleiadeans, Free will, look up, Holy Bible, Trident, I am the One,*
*Red carpet, Book of God, Mark of God, Balloons, My Heart, Burton (my grandfather's first name), Be prepared, Trudeau.*

*Have a good day my friend!*

*Mike*

# Chapter 16
# Will and Reason

God spoke of the great battle in the heavens and how our free will was lost:

> *"A long time ago, a great battle took place in the Heavens. Nothing was truthful, no one was understanding why this came to be. Once will was a shared thing but after the turmoil will was lost. Many others like Angels were needing to be guided. Angels and Archangels tried to help but they were not understanding the lost will."*

(J. Howard, *The Wisdom of God,* 2020, p10)

May 19th of 2022, I asked her in an email, this question for clarity:

*God said in your book, that "will" was lost and we lost a great part of our abilities or Knowledge. At least, I think that was the explanation. What is "will"? Intuition? Maybe another ability like the ability to use telepathy? Or something like the ability to make things move with our minds?? He explained that we would be able to help ourselves more with it. I'm just confused over the meaning.*

Johann answered me in a couple different emails and a blog post over the next couple of days.

*Good morning, Mike,*

*You ask good questions: the spirit, the will and the soul. These words may have been in capitals in the book because of the way God spoke about this in our earlier communications. At the time, I was teaching in a school which spoke about the 'great spirit' and I thought they meant through God or the Holy Spirit, so I spent much time untangling my cognitive dissonance. Let's start with the spirit; **the spirit** is energy that flows from one to the other but is not seen. For example, a person walks into a room of people and changes the mood of the group simply by arriving. The dynamics change, the energy is felt, and people pick up that feeling and* *respond to it (especially for the person who is the life of the party). In the sense of the Holy Spirit, it is the energy associated with God and the sacred, the sublime, the deities (Sophia, Archangels and maybe (?) some saints), and also felt in the voice of God, the word of God, the breath of God. (Walking in the woods with my son when he was a child he said "the forest is full of God's breath"). In old French 'esperit', today 'esprit' is like 'espirer' which means to breathe out. The spirit is unseen but felt and inspired. And so, there is evil spirit and good spirit.*

***The soul*** *is the being that is you and in you. It is the memory of past lives, experiences and the outcome/reaction. It is the heart memory, the heart rules over the brain, the memory is in the heart. Heart transplant recipients were studied and found to remember things not from them but from the previous doner. God said all is in the blood DNA, and this is pumped by the heart that is the seat of the soul. From previous lives the memory holds mostly of strong emotions, e-motion, movement of energy. Those who are demonically possessed have their soul trapped, the soul is guarded and the body controlled by an evil force.*

***The Will*** *is the sum of the two. The will puts into action, it is the faculty of conscious, deliberate choice and volition. The term "the will of the people" is very strong. (We need this now desperately). In the book, God speaks about the will as the action part of consciousness, spiritual inspiration and soul choices.*

And this:

*" Your question about **reason** is timely and all who are open to more truth settle with this important question. **Reason** has to do with opening to another answer that settles with the way answers as seen are wanted. Answers are only responses to **reason** and do not respond necessarily to truth, belief about a reality or evidence of proven truth. **Reason** only serves itself and does not open to the **will** which serves truth and opens to answer all who see it. The **will** helps truth move, **reason** well answers only to serve itself and serves to control a situation. An example of this is the **will truth** of why understood truth is being changed by **reasons** of used deceptions opening to control people and is more serving the **reason** givers. But all this folly is not of **will** but of **reason** proving the need to control.*

*Free will is what I give my children to better renew themselves and heal their soul. Lucifer uses self-serving reason to manifest the lies he wishes to spread among the Apoonancies' lies, forcing with fear, to make these lies believable. Be certain now all these lies will be dispelled. Many will serve with us and others to share knowledge of these coming days, and question all these lies serving beliefs on Earth. Here is the thing about lies and repetitive believed lies. As long as the lie is trusted, it lives as a symptom of this. But answering to greater truth with knowledge opens to the **will** and the **will*** *heals all as it stands alone as the truth does. And soon all this serving of lies falls apart and heals the trouble it caused and opens to a time of greater peace.*

*Good days are now coming and many know this in their hearts and ask many more questions to renew with us".*

*I think this is a good answer to your question. If you need more details, I will be happy to share. God said to me once, wait for the questions (because not all souls are capable of opening to truth).*

I still struggle with the definitions and the differences. I responded to her answers with an email describing events in my life that I thought I was using reason to handle. Message sent on May 27th, 2022:

*Good afternoon, Johanne!*

*Thank you for this response. I hope you don't take this the wrong way, but I am having a hard time with understanding this. You may have to provide me with more details. My life's successes and failures have all been the result of my choices, made with reasoning. I don't like to fail or be wrong in what I tell others. I wish to tell the truth and lead in the right direction. I study things well, hoping that when the hard decisions have to be made, that my reasons are well based. I understand what was written here about reason doesn't necessarily mean path to truth.*

*When I was about 12 or so, my mother had had enough of an abusive, alcoholic spouse. She took my siblings and I to my grandfather and demanded that he do something about his son, my father. That day, they committed him to alcohol treatment. When he was released, local people contacted him, befriended him and took him into their "fold," to help keep him away from the evil. Eventually, all of my family attended regular meetings of some level of Alcoholic Anonymous. I was in Ala-teen. Anyway, there we were all taught the Serenity Prayer. We recited it every meeting. I know it by heart. It asks for God's direction to guide us through hard decisions/choices through Wisdom. If the Will is the real truth, then it is what I seek to find.*

*My father had a hard life. He was deeply religious. He prayed daily and I now have his Bible, with all of his little prayers he had stuck in it. I have learned through my work on family history, how his torments started early. His Grandmother, my great grandmother was a very devout Catholic, attending masses every day until she couldn't anymore. My Grandmother, her daughter, I believe was under extreme pressure to produce either Nuns or Priests from her 5 children. The oldest daughter, left home at 16. I didn't know why, but she went to work and then college. My dad was next; he was sent to live with my grandfather's brother's family in Minneapolis when he was 14. They sent him to a Catholic boy's school with the intension of making him a Priest. He left after a semester and never went home but was raised by my grandmas' brother, a farmer and his wife. The next daughter was sent to a Convent at 12. She left before taking final vows and became a nurse. The next boy was sent to a seminary, but he became a barber, then an accountant. The last was raised at home and she is just seven years my senior. She told me once that her childhood was "hell", but I can only guess why, as she never said more. My dad learned to drink by hanging with the neighbor boys, but it got the better of him. He only had a 9th grade education and always felt that people thought he was dumb because of it. He felt he had let his parents down, too. Anyway, it was a long time of tormented life and he was about thirty-five when he stopped drinking. He struggled with that and seemed angry most of the time after. One thing I remember he said way back then, was that he didn't want his kids to have to work so hard as he did, to make ends meet. He wanted his children to be in office jobs, sitting at desks, rather than doing manual labor like his, a stone mason. So that drove me to seek a better life and to avoid the evil addictions. I did, but most of my siblings have struggled. I thought my reasoning ability was the difference and it could very well be, but, like you have answered my question, reasoning can be a false truth. Kind of a long story just to say that...........sorry for that!*

*I hope you can get the right words to fall into place as you write your blog. It must be hard work to develop things to say, but I am thinking you get some help! We just find so much peace and hope in your messages. Thank you for being our connection to truth!*

## The Serenity Prayer

God, grant me the serenity to accept the things I cannot change,

the courage to change the things I can

and the wisdom to know the difference.

# Chapter 17
# Dreams and Visions

There had been nothing significant to add to this story for a few months. Johanne and I exchanged occasional emails about a variety of topics for a time. That all changed in March of 2022. One morning, when I woke up, my wife was anxious to tell me something. She had a dream like nothing she had ever experienced before. On March 20, 2022, I emailed Johanne the details:

*Hello Johanne,*

*Nana had an interesting dream the other night. She described it as nothing like any dream she had dreamed before. She said her dreams usually just flow right along but this was in defined actions that quickly transitioned to the next "scene."*

*She was so anxious to tell me in the morning and couldn't wait for me to wake up. She kept asking me what it means (she just was trying to make sense of it all). I told her it was possibly a "vision" of things to come....*

*Her first scene started with us in a large "wooden" building. What she described had a wooden floor and walls and was open on one side. Somewhat like a large airplane hangar. The building was full of people. She said she only knew one other that was standing beside us and he was a former high school basketball coach we know. All the people were very quiet and not saying much and had high anxiety as they were attempting to contact family members to see if they were okay. They were all talking very low and no one was being loud. As we looked out of the open side (or doorway) it overlooked water. High over the water came thousands of triangular shaped ships, all tightly together in formation with lots of lights on them. She described the time of day around dusk as it was partly dark and the ships lights lit up the entire area. They traveled from the distant horizon and straight at us, passing over head. Thousands of them filled the sky, nearly touching and making no sound. She said, as they passed by, suddenly appearing in the sky was a huge cross, brightly shining. Then suddenly, she and I were standing outside a door to a (building/ room) (probably similar to the "air plane hangar type, she described first). She said I wouldn't go in but stayed just outside (she said I was waiting for someone). She said she stepped just inside and found a large gathering of people. Many were crying. She said they were all saying that they "accepted Jesus as their Lord and Savior." Then she awoke. She said she wasn't scared and was very peaceful. She was however, eager to tell me what a fantastic dream it was.*

*Later, I brought her to my computer and showed her some stealth jets and she thought the Chinese stealth jet looked the most like what she saw. It is very triangular and very close to the shape.*

*My research into modern "contact" with alien lifeforms points to the late 1940's and 1950's, with stories of US military getting alien technology in return for granting permission for them to "do scientific studies" on humans. So, it could be that the military has fashioned its hi-tech aircraft to be similar to alien. In your book, God described the ships as being like planets and pyramids. A couple of years ago, there was a US aircraft carrier that photographed and got video of triangular shaped objects flying over their ship for several minutes.*

*So, I believe she saw the alien version of the aircraft fly over in her dream/vision. I just talked to her about this again tonight and she remembers every detail, just like she told me the first time about 4 days ago.*

A couple of days later, Johanne responded:

> *Good morning, Mike and Nana,*
>
> *Mike I am happy to hear that your back is better. Nana, your dream was so amazing. Those ships are interesting, they are like TR3s, possibly back engineered as the ones Bob Lazar worked on. The hangar place where people gathered is also interesting. There is a quality of dreams that are more vivid, like a vision, and unforgettable. Nana, could you draw it, sketch the most important part of it?*
>
> *Mike, the pyramid ships are not in my book but maybe you know something I don't about this. I should check this in my questions, I don't think about those kinds of questions. But I once asked about these orbs that people are reporting and the extraordinary crop circles that appear in farmers' fields. God once said these were communication devices controlled off Earth and often used by the younger pilots who want to help people know they are there and wanting to warn humanity. Years ago, my son saw an orb in the yard late one night.*

She also replied a few days later on April 4, 2022 with an email and remarks about a couple of additional questions I had posed to her.

*Hi Nana and Mike,*

*Thank you so much for sharing this very descriptive dream. I can see it clearly. These are military ships. This is what God said about your dream: "These ships Nana has seen in her vision are being seen by us. These are military vessels from the United States, but these are used only as war machines, and these are more trouble than visited by ours coming. When these ships as seen by Nana's vision come, another group will follow and that crucifix of light with us is ours. We will arrive at the time of seeing these ships, and all these aircrafts will be dealt with. Their power sources will be stopped or disengaged which will cause these ships to fall to Earth and be dealt with. Be understanding we are not allowing these answers to war attacks anymore. And soon after, all power on Earth will be dealt with and some will be shut down, and soon after we will walk the Earth. You will open to another time on Earth, and many will see these eruptions of truth be dealt with, and many others will become answered by us in evidence of truth and shared knowledge".*

*About the pyramids, I was thinking the same thing as I was reading your words Mike. I need to reread the book. Some of the information is much more revealing about our present times. And you are right about the language; it is easier now. At first, it was difficult to discern but it has improved.*

*God made a promise. He is coming home. I hope I will meet both of you at the great celebration we will have when all evil is removed.*

*Johanne*

I replied back to her and said the following:

*Johanne,*

*Thanks for your (and God's) response to our email. There must be something going on as I heard this morning, that 3500 flights in the US were cancelled this last weekend, because of weather issues in our state of Florida. Then I heard that people were questioning that because why then would Alaska cancel lots of flights? They surely are not connected to Florida which is very far east and south of Alaska. The answer was because of pilot shortages! All hogwash, of course. Then I heard there were 600+ military flights in the air at the same time, which is double or triple to the normal 2-300. So military can fly but there is an issue with weather and pilot shortages for commercial flights!*

*I have been following MonkeyWerks, who gives reports via YouTube about 3 times a week. He gives a complete, worldwide report on air movements and significant moves he recognizes from his time in the military. He also has started showing cyber-attack software that shows who is attacking whom and satellite activity. It is very informative and usually lasts about 30 minutes a broadcast. He knows which kind of flights are troop or equipment movers, which are refueling planes, which are nuke "sniffers" and such. Unless someone watches this, they have no idea how the whole world is jockeying for position for a global war. It is scary.*

*A week ago, we had several of our children and families here for a birthday party for some of our little ones. Later, I told Nana that listening to these young adults was alarming to me as they didn't talk at all about world or economy issues, but more about their houses, their jobs and the little ones. Now, those conversations are well and good but like I told Nana, they do not have any idea how much danger there is and what is happening outside of their little worlds. They surely don't know how all will change soon.*

*Take Care and have a good day!*

*Mike M*

She followed up with this short response:

*It is probably better to say nothing to the younger ones, but to be there when needed. That is why you and Nana are the head of the family. (Reminds me of hiking up a mountain carrying 35 pounds of equipment, I mostly looked at my feet and not at the sky and the scenery.)*

The dreams were just starting.  Some were becoming quite real for Nana.   August 2$^{nd}$ of 2022 was an example.  I wrote to Johanne:

> *"Nana had another weird dream last evening and she described it to me, in detail, when she got up.  I usually "interview" her by asking all kinds of detailed questions and she usually comes through for me.  This dream generally had her frantically protecting young children from what she called "winged beasts".  I could not get much else for a description except that they were large.  She talked only about being in a building but couldn't say how big it was, but it was not a house.  She said that a couple of the children she was protecting seemed to be (I'll call it) possessed and she was able to recognize that they were already lost and she couldn't do anything about it.  She was very scared, terrified by the beasts and was doing her best to save the children. Then woke."*

Johanne responded with a comment, "The dream Nana had sounds frightening, I hope better dreams come her way."

Almost a month later to the day, on Sept 1$^{st}$, 2022, I wrote an email to Johanne reporting the latest "seeing" Nana had:

## Alien God

*Hello Johanne,*

*I will try to be brief here, but it's Nana and her dreams again………….. She told me this morning that she was awakened about 2:30 this morning by what she called a "form" that reached towards her with a "hand". As it got right in front of her face, she said she felt like it vacuumed out her (I'll call it her soul). She was "deposited" in a dark chamber or void. There she was met by her dear friend (who died about 15 years ago) and her grandmother (who died at about 100, a dozen years ago). They were all happy to see each other and they said they were so excited because they were getting ready to be with all of us again very soon. That this is really happening! Nana said she was very calm and not scared at all. Then suddenly, she awakened and said her heart was beating very fast and was sort of stunned by what had just happened and couldn't go back to sleep. That's all I got out of her as we are taking care of three of the grandkids for a couple days and she couldn't talk much. I will have more questions for her later when we get a chance to talk alone. She has a tendency to leave out details that I am able to get her to reveal with my multitude of questions I bring.*

*What do you think of that? At first, she talked about the darkness in the bedroom and not making out the form except for the hand that came to stop in front of her face. I worried a bit about that "darkness" reference and would have been happier hearing a reference to "light".*

*Mike*

The next day Johanne responded:

*Hi Mike,*

*The dream Nana had is interesting. Nana, you had no fear, which is telling. The vacuum part is disturbing to me because I felt this (years ago) when I stood by my mother's bed at her moment of death. It was so powerful that my arms fell in an open way as this occurred, as if a space was opened for her to leave. I remember God saying that death is not death, a soul lives on.*

*What is extraordinary is the way your family members were saying that they were getting ready to meet with you. This message is what God shares; we will be reunited with our families.*

*Nana, you are very open to the spiritual world, remember to call on God and Jesus if you feel fear. However, you seem to be well protected. Awesome dream!*

*All is as it should be. Be well.*

*Johanne*

It was several more months before Nana reported any more dreams or visions. On March 6th, 2023 something else occurred and I detailed this in an email to Johanne for her opinion.

*"This morning, Nana had an "experience" that was what I would call a "vision" and not a dream.*

*She said she had become aware that she was waking up from her sleep (seemed aware of her surroundings) but had not yet opened her eyes. Suddenly, she could see some men having some sort of discussion in a circle or semi-circle. She described them as being middle aged, bearded, seemingly from another time before this time. If that doesn't make sense, what I mean is that they seemed to be from 100 or 200 years ago, not from now, but before. Her first words to me about this was that she suddenly had the thought, "are these our family members finally coming with God?" She described the setting as outside, possible hilly country, and that her perspective was slightly higher than the group of men. She felt she was sitting on a side hill, just above the men and about 20 feet away. She also described the men as being larger than we are and that she could only see them from the waist up. She could see a few others that were farther away and she could never hear anything. One man she described as running away from the group with his hand held out and up, as if he were pointing out that "this is the way". She said all of this ended when suddenly a bright light was seen above and the whole vision vanished. She had opened her eyes at one point and it all disappeared, then she closed them and it continued. All of this lasted only about a minute. She looked at the time and it was about 6:45 am.*

*Nana says she had been praying so much lately, that God comes soon. She has been praying especially for children and worries about them being taken and abused.*

*I asked her to continue to think about the vision and see if she remembers any more detail. She told me it was such a short moment, lasting less than a minute, but she would think about it. I could tell she was intrigued and nervous about it but that she said it did not scare her."*

Johanne answered the next day and ask Nana for a few more details.

*"Nana's dream is interesting. It is as if she was seeing some kind of discussion or meeting. Between the time of waking and actually being awake seems to be a time for this kind of experience. I am not a dream specialist but I had similar experiences where I was listening to a voice of a woman speaking to me, informing me of something I could not remember, and this lasted 3 weeks. Weeks later the same experience was repeated except it was a male voice. My interpretation of this was my soul receiving instructions. Nana, do you remember anything else from your experience?"*

Nana sent the following back after some more thought was given:

> *"As far as my recent experience that Michael described for you, I just want you to know this was like nothing I have ever experienced before! I was absolutely awake. In the moment before I would normally open my eyes, this "picture" appears with the men talking. I wondered right away, what is this? I tried to open my eyes to see if I was really awake or even in my own home but as I opened my eyes slightly, it was dark and gone. Then when I closed my eyes again, there it was. The group was about 15- 20 or so and they were in a staggered circle of small groups, then sometimes as a whole group in the discussion. I studied their faces to see if I knew anyone but did not. I was not frightened and they were being friendly to each other and just having a discussion, except for the one that was running in the distance that was pointing towards the spot where the bright light appeared. It flashed so bright, then everything was gone. The flash was like an electric spark, burning so bright, which absorbed the whole scene into itself and it was gone. Then I opened my eyes and I felt calmness and very hopeful and had the thought that God is coming.*
>
> *Thank you for what you do with the blog and such and of course, the many emails we've exchanged. I pray often for the safety of our family and especially the little ones. All children, not just our family."*

On the 4th of April, 2022, Johanne answered us back. She had this to say:

*Hi Nana,*

*Your vision was intense. Thank you for sharing this with me. I asked about this today in my communication and this is the response: "She sees the truth of our words". To me this also means you are able to see past the veil. The fact that you were not afraid and trusted their demeanor gives me hope as well.*

*The communication today was directed to God's children and I will try to post this later. I believe we are here to witness and participate in the return of God and His son Jesus. These are truly exciting times and a good reason to be hopeful no matter how bleak these times seem. It's been difficult for good people on Earth for a long time, but I believe things are about to change drastically. There is an end to evil, and then we will have a great celebration.*

*Stay focused on God's and Jesus' return home. Be one with God.*

*Johanne*

Special Note:   About a year later, I asked Nana if she remembered that dream with the group of men, and she did.  I asked if she noticed one that seemed to be the leader of this "meeting" and she replied that she did and then I said, "you may have seen the face of God."

About 6 weeks later, Nana had a troubling dream and I described it in another email to Johanne. On May 14th, I wrote an email and detailed several questions for Johanne and a short paragraph on this last dream:

> *"She said to me this morning, that she awakened from a "nightmare" in the early morning hours, about snakes somehow, bringing children to the devil. One of the children was her oldest granddaughter and she was fighting her great fear of snakes to get to save her granddaughter. I asked, "What did the devil look like?" She said like a snake but he was standing up in the front. (I took that as probably like a King Cobra stands tall) and that was it…..we didn't talk about it much more except she said she awoke with her head pounding and her heart racing."*

Nana had a few more significant dreams or visions in the next few months with this one being the one that scared her the most. It was now June 18th, 2024. I emailed Johanne the story:

*"Nana had an episode early this morning that frightened her. She woke me about 5:30 am to tell me what she dreamt/saw.*

*She began by telling me she had not been dreaming and suddenly she could see the sky and she saw a ship (I will describe in a bit) that went up and away from her. that she said it was the same as the one she has seen before during the day, near our home. She described the ship (vaguely) as being a disk shape, silvery and had some blue lights on it. She said that it appeared, then disappeared. She had the thought that "oh, that's how they do that", as if she understood at that moment. What scared her was that suddenly, a being/person appeared to her about 6 feet away, noticeably larger than us, with dark hair. It told her that they would come for her tomorrow night, she thought it said as it left. She immediately woke me and was frightened that someone was coming to take her and her first thought was "but, what about my family??". She was visibly shaken and thinks now that something is coming to get her. I assured her that what they might have been wanting to tell her is that they are coming, not to take her away but, to arrive."*

The craft or ship seen by her was not the first or last time. She has routinely seen this particular object many times during day hours and will be described later in this book.

She had three other times during the period of 2023 and 2024, that she described visitors appearing in our bedroom during the night. Once she claimed that she opened her eyes to see three figures standing near the foot of our bed. We had 3 grandchildren staying overnight and they were sleeping in her bed (I was in another room). She thought two looked like her son and son-in-law and the other had a mustache and she didn't recognize him. Suddenly she realized or determined they were of a dark source and realized her granddaughter could see something also. She suddenly sat up in bed looking in that direction and then they disappeared. Another time she woke to see multiple "beings" leaning over me on my side of the bed and looking at her. Then there was one that I wrote to Johanne about in mid-October of 2024:

> *About two weeks ago, she was awakened and felt like someone was staring at her. She sat up and could make out a very tall being, standing in the corner of the bedroom. Scared at first, she called out my name (I was in another room). She said she suddenly got calm, was not afraid and reached over and turned on the light next to the bed and it wasn't there. She claims it was roughly 7.5 to 8 feet tall, and could not see the face clearly but it was wearing a long cloak. She maintains that she was not afraid after the initial moment she saw it. I stood where she said it was and she claimed it was about 2 feet taller than me.*

Johanne answered as part of another email a couple of days later and this surprised me with what she had to say:

> *Yesterday, my son told me he had a seeing (in his bedroom) of a cloaked tall being and as soon as he tried to focus on it, it disappeared. He thought it was his eyes playing tricks on him. What are these beings? I have no idea, I hope they are friendly. Like you, I see nothing.*

The last one and most recent vision or dream reported to me was in early 2026 and was of her and other women leading several groups of children down a corridor (much like you would see in a school situation). They all entered a large room as if they were taking the children to a safer place.  She described seeing in that large room, a group of very tall, slender, pale skinned "beings," standing around another that appeared dead and was lying on the floor or a platform. The beings asked them to come with their group and Nana replied something like, "God is my one true God and I will not follow you ever or let any of these children go with you………… none of us helping the children will!"  Then she reported that suddenly, all of the beings were sucked out of a hole that appeared in the wall and she woke up.

In October of 2024, my grandson, who is a researcher in his own right with his own drive to find answers to things he doesn't understand, contacted me and I wrote about it in an email to Johanne on the 26th:

*Hi Johanne,*

*I got a text from my 16-year-old grandson about an hour ago and he asked if he could call me to tell me about his dream last night. Before I could answer, he called me. He was very excited about what he saw and wanted me to know every detail. He started out by saying he saw God defeat Lucifer. He started at the end of the story and filled me in on things that led up to the finale.*

*I'm going to attempt to write this out as he said it to me. Nana was sitting beside me on the sofa and she heard all of it also.*

*First, he started………..''Hey Grandpa, Grandpa……..I had a crazy dream last night and I saw God defeat Lucifer and it was over in like 5 seconds or less!'' He repeated that a few more times. I asked how it happened. He said that he and some friends were by a mountain and he saw a strange looking cloud come down from the sky. Suddenly, it was God, or Jesus (he said he didn't know which one it was but, he had long hair) and it was over in a few seconds. Lucifer was crying from the loss and he eventually faded away to a skeleton, then to nothing and it was over. And, all of his followers were gone. I asked what he looked like. He said he looked human, was well built, light complected but had green eyes and curly, medium length, brown hair. He also was shirtless but wearing pants. I asked what did God look like. He just described him as having long, brown hair and also light complected but his hair was definitely longer than Lucifer's. He also said a couple times, that he wasn't sure if it was God or Jesus. He did blurt out as I pressed him about what destroyed Lucifer and he said, "I don't think it was God who destroyed Lucifer, but I think it was the Holy Spirit," but it was over in seconds. As I asked more questions, he started filling in a back story leading up to this moment he witnessed. He talked about not being able to buy anything at a gas station. He said he was hungry and had cash but they wouldn't accept it. Another person walked up with items and they scanned his forehead and he paid that way. I asked him at that point if he had ever heard of the mark of the beast. He said he had and then I explained that one of the ways they were going to limit us was to only let us buy and sell things if we had the mark in or on our hand or forehead. Then he said that Lucifer had tried to convince him to come with him and that he was promised anything he wanted but my grandson denied him and said that he would not follow him. He repeated in astonishment how quickly he was dispatched by God and the Angels when they descended upon him. He described how as soon as Lucifer was gone, the whole world changed and everything was much nicer.*

*He's coming over to my house in a couple of days to help me lift some things to put away for winter and I will try and ask him some more details and will pass them on if I get anything new. He said it was weird that he usually doesn't remember his dreams but the two vivid ones as this one and one other, that I think I wrote to you about last year, where he described everyone taking the medicine but him and one neighbor and the others were all jumping into a huge firepit or something like that………. because a minister told them to.*

*I thought I had better write this tonight while it was still fresh. Hope you are doing well. Are you working on your other book yet? I'm about 2/3rds of the way through your other book again and only get a few chapters read before I need to work on other projects. I am amazed at how I find things written that seems like it's the first time I've come across them, even after reading the book at least 4 times!*

*Take Care,*

*Mike M*

Johanne responded with this on November 8th, 2024:

*Hi Mike,*

*How are you?*

*This is a quick response to your grandson's dream from God, as I just asked about it. He said: "His dream was correct, but it will not come to pass about the money exchange. Only a few want this to happen, and it will be stopped, and this evidence of truth will be ended. The stories of the Book of Revelation are only settling with the plan, as the seeing of this will be stopped. Be certain, we can stop all in an instant. Be serving with us soon."*

*It is amazing that your grandson was connecting this way through his dream. Stay in contact with God and His family, and all will improve when They return to Earth.*

*Talk to you later my friend.*

*Johanne*

# Chapter 18
# Ships and Crafts

*"These ones ask many questions about the sightings of UFOs. See this now and understand many people observe ships in the sky. These are our ships and these evident ships are preparing to land and disembark only at the right time. Be understanding there is nothing to fear. We are coming home.*
*Be renewing with us soon and be ready to answer to my call." God*
J. Howard, <u>The Wisdom of God</u>, Blog 10-28-2023)

As mentioned in the previous chapter, Nana saw a craft in one dream she had.  It was not the first time she saw one and had several encounters during that day and over a period of years.  Her last sighting was in the fall of 2025, in eastern South Dakota, as she traveled on the interstate.  She saw three together, of the exact same ship she had continued to see over the last three years. We will now go through the first and continuing times of her observations.

On the first of December 2023, I wrote with excitement about something that Nana had seen.

*Nana had been at her daughter's house, who lives 4 blocks to our south after she returned from dealing with the newborn's family in another city. She forgot her purse at her daughter's house and returned to get it, towards nightfall. Where her daughter lives there are several new houses being built. As that street fills in as the last lots still undeveloped in our neighborhood. Nana was just a half block away from her daughter's house and in an open area not filled with homes. She noticed a disc-shaped object to the right and above her daughter's house, only about twice as high as the house. She said she pulled over and stopped to watch it move from her right to her left across the street in front of her. Suddenly, as if a veil was pulled back, a structure, including a much larger disc, connected to the first disc appeared. Scared but curious, she pulled up the street to her daughter's drive and rolled her window down. She had called me by this time and she was trying to describe what she saw. She wanted me to try to catch a look at it but the terrain and other homes blocked my view from my home. I suggested a helicopter but she claimed it made no noise, so I then said, "hot air balloon?". She denied that and said it was NOT! This craft moved over the river that is very close by and started following that general direction. I quizzed her at length when she got back to the house and she described it as the size of about 3 large houses together and very lit up so she could see the entire craft. It had some red and blue lights on it but mostly was just bright "white" light, illuminating the entire unit. She tried to draw it but that is not a strength for her. I asked if it looked like the "Enterprise" from the Syfy "Star Trek" series and she didn't have any idea what I was talking about. She is not into science fiction stuff.........Anyway, we looked at some pictures on the internet and she said that it kind of looked like that. She attempted to draw it again and it had some similarities to the 'Star Trek" ship. Small disk in front, connecting to a larger disc that was lower on the structure. She said it didn't frighten her but she was scared of being "abducted". I told her I thought I might know what it is. I said Gersiels. I explained they were to come first and would clean our water. That explains to me the reason for following the river that runs by our home. She was only about 500 feet from this thing the whole time.*

*Now, going back to last month, I told you she had seen a couple of things that looked similar to airplanes but were different than this. Of all of her sightings, the crafts have always been near this river system. This recent sighting was 2 days ago. Yesterday, she had an appointment at a business located about 5 miles west of our home. She said she was driving west and saw a sunny reflection in the distance and there again, was the craft she had seen the night before! This was broad daylight, middle of the day. She said it was exactly what she saw that night. Again, it was near the same river system that winds through our city. So, with that new sighting, I told her that this is too frequent and they seem to be closer to her than the initial ones. I said they may be trying to get closer to her and to not try to hide. Obviously, she sees things that most do not. She complained that she wished I was with her at least once so she didn't think it was so weird that she is seeing these and she is always alone when it happens. I don't know if I am right or not but I told her not to fear them as any contact now should be with "good" ones.*

Johanne replied with this:

*Hi Mike and Nana,*

*Congratulations to your family on the new arrival. So happy to see growing families.*

*Nana your sightings are amazing. There seems to be many sightings these days. Nothing to be afraid of, God said this would happen just about the same time the wars in the Middle East would erupt. So, it's all happening now. It is even hard for me to imagine what all this looks like. But here we are, what an interesting time to be living through even though the sufferings are great in times of war. "All is now" were His recent words.*

Johanne wrote in her blog, a message from God from August 2023:

*August 4, 2023: "Know now these truths about who shares knowledge with whom. These people who see these ships around Earth with their telescopes are seeing these ships circling Earth, but they see only a few who are caught in view. Evidence of these ships are serving with us, and are serving another seen response to knowledge of our bridging truth. These servants of truth are better seen as lights in the sky. These are ships responding to another group of Aliens and these are the Gersiels. They arrive first with evidence of their answer to not harm but also to remove the poisons put on Earth by the Reptilians, and they arrive to clean the waters on Earth as arrivals become seen. They are kind and friendly, yet very strong and wise, and they will see to the protection of the innocent humans, children and living beings on Earth.*

*These are the first to land on Earth to share knowledge with humans in evidence of the time believed to be the arrival of Aliens. More good people come after and these are the Settlers. You may be renewing with some who are present on Earth without your knowledge because they are mostly human looking. They are capable of greater helping ways, with greater truth and greater healing ways. Be seeing how all starts with the arrival of the Gersiels who will actively share how they must prepare all with the understandings of our bridging ways before we arrive".*

(J. Howard, <u>The Wisdom of God</u>, Blog 10-18-2023)

Having had several discussions with Nana over time, about the exact details of what she saw, I can give a rough description of the shape. As explained, it was a small disk and a larger disk connected with a framework of "arms". After I had drawn what she felt was closest to what she saw, it did indeed look like a later version of the starship "Enterprise". From what I had drawn, I could see how it was possibly a ship that was a disk-shaped unit, which could separate and extend with these arms from a "stackable" position to an open extension by separating the two discs horizontally. Like two dinner plates stacked and then moved and placed side by side. All of the sightings came within yards of a river system.

In August of 2022, I wrote to Johanne and told her about my second father-in-law's experience as a child.

*I don't know if I told you this, but my ex-father-in-law was very interested in UFOs. About 25 years ago, when he was about in his 70's, he and I were sitting alone in their small "den", watching TV and visiting. He noticed I had glanced down at his UFO themed book and magazines laying on the floor next to his chair and he asked if I believed in UFOs. I said I believe there must be life out there as there is high probability that life would have existed out in all that space. Then he told of when he was 10 or 12 years old and was helping his grandfather clean up an old building. He happened to walk out a back door and suddenly, a very large "ship" floated slowly by, not making a sound as it travelled out of sight. He said it was only about 50 feet above the ground and he was frozen in fear. He realized his grandfather was next to him by the time the ship had disappeared. When he turned to his grandfather, the old man asked if he saw that? He told him, "yes", then the old man said, "Never tell anyone what you just saw and if you need to talk about it, then talk to me." The rest of his life, he tried to find out more and was obsessed with getting his hands on anything that would talk about UFO's. I don't know where his soul is today but I believe he is happy to know much more about what happened that day, when he was just a little boy.*

I sometimes think I wished he could have been here for the "seeing of many ships in the sky" as he has been gone for many years now. He was a WW2 veteran and was one of the first of the troops to land in Japan after the atomic bomb had been dropped. If what you are reading in this book is true, then he already knows and that makes me happy.

Another story is much fresher and comes only a little over a year ago. I relayed this to Johanne in an email on July 14, 2025:

*Hi Johanne,*

*I have an interesting story for you about my young granddaughter.*

*Last year, when she was but 2 years old, her family was visiting us. One day she "disappeared" and I went looking for her. I found her in our master bedroom with a permanent marker and she had drawn a shape on a white blanket. Nana was subdued but I knew she was furious that she had done that, but kept her calm. Her mom, my daughter, scolded the little one for doing the damage. Nana took the item and tried washing it out but to no avail. We have used it as a covering for a bench at the foot of the bed.*

*Here we are, a year later, and I was making the bed a couple of days ago, and I noticed the "art work" again. I studied it. My first thought was a spaceship, then, maybe a dog. I know how littles draw funny-shaped people and animals. That got me thinking; what was she drawing and why haven't I ever questioned it before. I knew it wasn't just random pen strokes.*

*Yesterday, I texted my daughter. I sent a picture of the "art work" and said, "what do you think she drew that time?" In a couple minutes, she responded, after showing this picture to her daughter and asking her. The reply was, "a rocket ship". My daughter thought that was funny. I said that I thought it was a spaceship or a dog. Then I asked her to ask the little one, "what are all the dots?" And she replied, "all the little ships".*

*She is only just turned 3 a month ago. How does a little one know about rocket ships and different sizes of them??*

*Have a good day,*

*Mike Maher*

Many interesting things can be learned from these new souls if you spend some time talking with them. Johanne responded that "The fact that she drew all the little ships is surprising."

What I have presented here are first person accounts of sightings and knowledge of crafts and ships. We also have messages received from God to Johanne, with some written in a book and others on a blog. All connect. As I have been putting these puzzle pieces together for you to read about, I watched live, an interview on television just days ago and this is what was the transcript of the conversation:

**Martha MacCallum interview of Anna Paulina Luna, Congresswoman representing Florida.**

**Feb 20, 2026**

> ***MacCallum:*** *Question is buzzing around a lot this week. Are we alone in the universe? So here's what President Obama said that got all of this back in the headlines.*

> ***Podcast Interviewer to Obama:*** *Are aliens real?*

> ***Obama:*** *Uh, they're real, but I haven't seen them. And and and uh they're not being kept in uh what is it? Area 51. Area 51. there there's no underground uh facility unless there's this enormous conspiracy and they they hid it from the president of the United States*

> ***MacCallum:*** *Um so he later said the chances that we have been visited by aliens is low.*

> ***Obama:*** *I saw no evidence during my presidency that they had made contact with us.*

> ***MacCallum:*** *He was you know, suggesting that he was joking uh and having some fun with the podcaster in that particular instance*

*Here's President Trump though when he got a question about what President Obama said on Air Force One from* **Peter Ducey:** *Barack Obama said that aliens are real. Have you seen any evidence of nonhuman visitors to Earth?*

**Trump:** *Well, he gave classified information He's not supposed to be doing that, you know So, aliens are real. Well, I don't know if they're real or not. I can tell you he gave classified information. He's not supposed to be doing that. So, that got a lot of attention.*

**MacCallum:** *Hours later, the president posting on Truth Social that he's directing the release of government files related to alien and extraterrestrial life and UFOs. He wants everything to come out that the government has on this. So, with that, we bring in Republican Congresswoman from Florida, Anna Paulina Luna. She is chair of the oversight committee task force on the declassification of federal secrets. She has said that there is evidence of interdimensional beings that can operate through the time spaces that we currently have, which is obviously um going to catch a lot of people's attention. Um Anna Paulina Luna, thank you very much, Congressman. It's good good to have you with us today. Um so you I want to go back to that. You told Joe Rogan in a podcast in August when you were discussing all of this that you have viewed evidence of interdimensional beings here on Earth and that they operate through the time spaces that we currently have. Can you explain what you mean by that?*

**Luna:** *Yeah. Um I think that a good example would be some of the photo visual evidence that we've seen directly in some of these classified briefings that will now be made public. Um, one of the famously now, uh, I guess infamous videos that we showed in one of our hearings was actually a video that was dead dropped to Eric Berles, who's a member of Congress, um, from within the Department of War, and it shows a UAP, an unidentified aerial phenomenon deflecting a Hellfire missile. Um, this was ca taken off of ISR footage off the coast of, I believe it was Yemen. Um, so long story short, there have been briefings that we've received as Congress that leads us to believe that yes, there is definitely an advanced technology out there that's not created by mankind. And yes, of course, we've seen other evidence where it could potentially be UAPs and then we later find out that there's drones, but there is a certain amount of evidence that we simply can't explain. um some of the physics that are defied in how these vehicles operate um are very interesting to note and we are not the only government that's you know looked into this extensively but I really do look at this from a lens of national security and as you know as we continue to evolve specifically on the front of AI and drone technology um we have to ensure that a are these things whatever they may be are they potential adversarial uh weapons advanced weapons or not and I think the whole aspect that the federal government can deny access to members of Congress of which has happened not just to myself but to other members of Congress as well is not* *just alarming uh but it's also something that cannot truly exist in free and fair society. Government should not operate in secrecy. And so I look forward to the American people being able to determine their own conclusion after they've seen some of the evidence that we have seen. Uh but most recently, Representative Gates actually came forward. He was on that initial Codel with me and Representative Tim Burchett where we we were denied access and uh he will tell you that if you've seen some of the stuff that we've seen you will too become a believer.*

**MacCallum:** *So I mean it's it's fascinating and you know so you're saying that the Air Force has covered up UAP sightings. So, you know, if there is potentially is it because it's technology that we have that they don't want anyone to know that we have militarily or is it that it's a foreign actor who has some abilities in technology and things that spin in ways that we can't understand?*

**Luna:** *Based on our interviews that we've conducted, not just in person, but also to um given some of the testimony that we've received, we do have reason to believe that this tech is not created by mankind. However, it is also possible that there are certain advanced weapons that the US government may have that they're denying us access to. But here's the problem. when you have unelected bureaucrats denying access to members of government that are supposed to oversee and write the checks for that federal spending and then we're* *also getting reports that there are people being threatened whether it be physically whether there have been you know interesting deaths associated with people that have been coming forward as whistleblowers which has been brought up in some of the testimony that we've received not just myself but you saw recently there was a movie that came out "The Age of Disclosure" um where this is also referenced now by the secretary of state Marco Rubio um this is one the most bipartisan and bicameral things in Washington DC. And so we we definitely are looking forward to sharing this and and explaining this further with the American people.*

***MacCallum:*** *Anna Paulina Luna, Congresswoman, thank you. It's fascinating and uh I think we all want to know more about this. I think it's sort of tripped back into the uh into the universe, so to speak, with um sort of an off-handed comment by President Obama that turned into something deeper and now we may get some more disclosures. Uh we'll see. At least there's pressure for it. Thank you so much.*

# Chapter 19
# The Book of Enoch

In the Holy Bible, Enoch is mentioned.

> *"And Enoch lived sixty and five years, and begat Methuselah. And Enoch walked with God after he begat Methuselah three hundred years, and begat sons and daughters. And all the days of Enoch were three hundred sixty and five years. And Enoch walked with God; and he was not, for God took him"* (Genesis 5:21–24).

Enoch was the great grandfather of Noah.  He lived a relatively short existence when compared to the others in his genealogical lines by only attaining an age of 365 years, "when he then walked with God and was no more". One of only two individuals listed in the Bible of having never died, but taken away. Elijah was the other. Little is said about him but he is believed to be the author or at least the inspiration of the Book of Enoch and is sometimes referred to as the "scribe" of judgement. The Book of Enoch is not found in any Protestant nor Catholic versions of the Holy Bible. It is, however, found in the Ethiopian Bible. It is important to point out here and again in the next chapter, that many books were not included in the "final" version of the Bible. The Book of Enoch was believed to be not mainstream enough and had content that contradicted some of what was in the final version of the "good" book.

Johanne had suggested I read this work as a way for me to gain a better understanding of who the Nephilim, the Watchers and the Fallen Angels were. Luckily, the video she pointed me to was a great resource for me. It was a 4-hour narration of the 5 parts of the document. I would recommend it as something to know, in addition to a general knowledge of the Holy Bible and to go with things included in this book and in The Wisdom of God by Johanne Howard.

The five sections were:

- **The Book of the Watchers:** Details the fallen Angels (led by Semjaza and Azazel) who descend to Earth, mate with human women, teach forbidden arts (alchemy, weaponry and sorcery), and father the destructive Nephilim who are giant beings of a cannibalistic nature. Enoch also warns the Watchers of their judgment.

- **The Book of Parables:** Focuses on end-times, featuring revelations about a "Son of Man" who will judge the wicked and reward the good in a restored world.

- **The Astronomical Book:** Contains Enoch's visions of the laws governing the sun, moon, stars, and the calendar. He is taught the mechanics of the celestial body movements.

- **The Book of Dream Visions:** Covers a history of the world from the fall of Angels, through the flood, to the final kingdom arrival.

- **The Epistle of Enoch:** Offers warnings to future generations regarding the paths of righteousness and wickedness.

I notified Johanne of my finishing the Enoch video on January 30, 2023.

*On Saturday, I finally finished listening to the video attachment about Enoch that you sent in our last email. I have listened to a shorter version before, but in this one, I was very interested in the descriptions of the movement of the sun and the moon.*

She replied:

> *I find that in this version of the book of Enoch; I recognize God and Uriel. My first messages came from Uriel in 2003. He showed me how to communicate with him, and started to teach me some words in their language, it's fascinating how this all happened. You understood what was said about the movement of the sun and the moon, I found this part difficult to follow.*

Then a few weeks later, I noticed something she had posted on some of her blogs about the Fallen Angels. I brought up two examples that I was having trouble understanding who these "Angels" were.

> Message from October 20th, 2023: *"Now be visited by questions opening to another truth. Be certain all serves with us and others as we descend onto Earth. Be understanding how all becomes well believed by the trusted ones who understand who we are. Be understanding also who shares knowledge and light of understanding with us because these "Aliens" respond to our ways.*
> *Evidence of our ways does more to share knowledge with people than to answer to another way of control. Better to see this evidence of knowledge at our time of meeting than to fear another control system. And be certain, we are only opening more on Earth now because my*

*children seeing to our ways is truth. And those who oppose us, and these liars, will be dealt with.*

*Be visited soon by us and know we are seeing all truth serve, and trust with us will be easy as arrivals are seen. Be understanding how all opens to shared knowledge now. Be understanding we are settling with bridging ways very soon and renewing with a time of great answers and better days answering to my children.*

*More bridging times come at the time of greater truth, better answers and trust in knowledge of who we are and why we are dealing with this now and only now.*

*All these ways are serving only now because you see the evidence of these rulers of Earth destroying everything and blame is put on those who suffer these responses to pollution caused by these liars and thieves.*

*These ways of destruction and blame will be stopped at the time believed to be Armageddon which renews with WW3 and the final war. And this is only well serving these rulers who open to Lucifer and other demons you call Archons or the* **fallen Angels.**

*These demons were never Angels and this you need to see at the time of revelation opening more now. These demons are serving Lucifer and are entranced in a hivemind serving only one master and this only, as serving with us never existed.*

*Be understanding this too is a lie. No one who serves with us has ever shared knowledge with these devils. We are united and have always been but some were taken from us. And so was Sophia who will soon be free, and her memories will be serving a time of restoration and*

*healing with us where she belongs. All comes soon now, be certain of my words". God*
(J. Howard, <u>The Wisdom of God,</u> Blog 10-21-23)


And another written in December:

Message from God, December 13, 2023:

*" Be renewing with us soon and renew with the many truths at the time of better trust in who we are. Answers as said are here. All who are settling with lies know of the greater problems with the coming events, and they are responding to more than indoctrination.*
*They respond to the evil in them. These truths are serving with their own choices and not because they are serving with proof of lies. These followers of darkness are seeing to their own ways, and this only serves them. More troubles answer them as their master Lucifer is angered with their failures.*
*Now see these ones be trusted by no one and how their plans are destroyed as it was before in Babylon. They answered to blasphemy and answered to the way of the dealers of lies. And now all opens to answer their deaths an avenged murder.*
*Tell yourselves this is what they see as better justice but it is only murder and thievery.*
*Q. Who are "they"?*
*A. These are the ones called Zionists and governments in evidence of what position they hold. But most as said,*

*have infiltrated governments to plan their takeover to better serve their plans of destruction of all societies to make their ponders of world dominance.*

*You will see these plans believed to answer the rich and impoverish the serfs. They will only respond to better serve themselves. This was the plan made with the* **fallen Angels** *a very long time ago. They will not succeed; they are serving their end now. Their time is over and they will fall one by one.*

*Then all will begin to be better with evidence of greater answers than ever seen before the darkness ruled on Earth. And this was the time of light and wisdom, with greater truth and enlightenment. And this time opens to another time, and another renewal of responding truth.*

*Be ready to answer to greater eruptions of days of darkness being dealt with, and see the veil of lies become lifted. And understand the truth of how all becomes well answered in evidence of these last days of darkness.*

*Be ready to be with us and be free of all torment. This is a promise I made and I will keep. And now is the time to be reunited". God*

(J. Howard, <u>The Wisdom of God,</u> Blog 12-15-23)

She responded on the 6th of January, 2024 with this as part of a larger email:

*Your question confused me a bit, but I think I can sort this out. The way I understand these words, God uses the information we were given by humans to explain the "fallen Angels" or "Archons". However, these entities are not from God or heaven. Lucifer is not a son of God. Lucifer and his demons came to Earth, "fallen from the sky" meaning spaceships. The use of the word "angel" was used to describe their powers to humans. They are hivemind beings who may have been created by Lucifer to serve him. Lucifer is a conqueror and a destroyer. He wants to be like God and rule over many planets. He destroyed Mars. Not only that, but he has destroyed every planet he set foot on. He is doing it now as God and his armies are returning to Earth. Lucifer wishes to destroy all life, now calling it carbon pollution and blaming all on humans, animals and now trees. They took over Earth, attacking and destroying, and causing the beings who were here, to engage in a great war. Many escaped and many were left behind, becoming slaves to this new order. In order to get the slaves to obey, these parasite demons possessing humans, made themselves to be the representatives of God. Because those who are God's children have a deep-rooted connection to God, and the need of these demons was to control all beliefs and thoughts to achieve a hivemind. This is how I understand it, it is similar to the stories of Atlantis and Lemuria. This is why God keeps telling us that He has truths to open to with us. The Bible is not the whole truth; it is a series of stories that does not tell the whole truth. Recently, I reread the book of John from the scrolls found in urns in the 1940s Nag Hammadi caves, who tell nasty lies about the Sophia being saying she created monsters. I asked God about this, believing it was true hidden scripture, and His answer was, these are more lies told to confused people. The powers that should not be are great deceivers who have absolutely no limits, and these lies have been going on a very long time. Trust your heart and only this.*

# Chapter 20
# Bible Talk

To paint a more complete picture of what we are experiencing here, we need to talk about the Bible. I have commented many times to others, that the Bible was written by men. You must understand that the document has gone through multiple changes over thousands of years and who knows how many iterations there really has been. I have read that there were well over 700 books written and considered for inclusion, some even after being included for hundreds of years, suddenly got removed.

Originally, some of the Old Testament stories date back to about 800 BC with the New Testament being written between the first and 4th century AD. More than 40 authors are recognized for the current versions and it could be the work of hundreds more. The Bible was the first book printed after the invention of the printing press in 1455. Prior to that for hundreds of years, Bibles were hand copied, line by line, page by page, mostly by monks in monasteries. Were mistakes made? Were words and sentences revised to suit the writer better with their own interpretations? Who might know the truth about these things? In the end, the common number of books in the Bible is 66, with one or two more in some versions. I have seen comparisons of the same verses in multiple versions and printings, to have significant changes in one or two words, that can completely change the meaning of the statement. So, change continues today.

I am not a Bible scholar. The Bible readings used in church are very familiar to me but I haven't studied it that much. It was always an intension of mine to read the whole Bible but that never has happened. For some reason for most of my life, I have concentrated on what is written in Genesis and in Revelations. That's right. The beginning and the end. It all goes back to me just wanting to know what is happening. Why is it this way? How will it end?

God had these things to say about our Holy Books:

*"Trusting in the spiritual world can be difficult because humans have been in darkness so long. You have an ancestor of a superior source of life. You are the result of many thousands of years of unrealized strength.*

*Awakening to the potential will make many serve others who will act as false prophets. You must then only be serving yourself towards your knowledge and awakening.*

*The way to do this is so simple, and demands the courage of your heart to do this. Understanding the way of God is all written before for all to find and discern the right from the wrong. In the Bible, in the Torah and in the Koran. You must discover your secrets in these books because these books alone have the tree of life written in them for all to understand and be stopping the wars and destruction of the Earth. Will you read them and see for yourself?"*

(J. Howard, <u>The Wisdom of God,</u> 2020, p. 4)

*"Be seeing that the holy books on Earth, are written to open too many truths used because I wanted my words to be heard by you, and opened these words to your Setu way. These books became reformed by those who manipulated my words, and because well controlled information fell into the hands of demons, my words were changed and served to enrich them, and create slavery of all sorts. These ways are not ours and never were and now you must open to our time to walk the Earth. The evidence of who we are heals you, as we are soon descending onto Earth in great numbers.*

*Be serving a time of deep meditation, and try to respond to my words in your heart, know we are soon reunited, as we are together as families are. Be ready and serve answers to your own truth in evidence of our time to be reunited. Now, we are so pleased to be coming back to Earth to re-awaken all of our family members to the better truth."*

(J. Howard, <u>The Wisdom of God,</u> 2020, p. 47)

*"Be well renewing with us and be happy to meet with your families soon, as they are soon happy to see you again. Be serving with us soon and be healing all the harm that has been imprinted on your hearts to stop you from knowing the whole truth. Be seeing that half-truths can be misleading as lies and know that your holy books are changed by many half-truths. You must learn to be very discerning at reading these words written by men with the desire of control on their minds. Be ready for the truth as you meet with us. See for yourselves who we are and why we are angry about the abuse of Earth, as no good laws are made to heal the victims and serve only the elite who are renewing with more power and greed."*

(J. Howard, <u>The Wisdom of God,</u> 2020, p. 241)

And once again, Johanne presented in her blog, God's message about the Bible and other holy books, in her own words:

*Now God did not choose to connect with many people of power who claim God chose them. God is not responsible for all the stories and historical "facts" or written rhetoric in the Bible. God did not tell anyone to blindly follow or believe any religious book or leader. God was not in Constantinople around the year 325 to decide what was being accepted to make the Bible. Emperor Constantine directed this endeavor with the council of Nicea, in part to regain power, resolve discord and unite the people.*

*God did say, in these communications I received, to find the truth in these books of religion (like the Bible, the Torah, the Quran, etc.). Use your critical thinking, read them and sort it out yourself; what is believable, what is not and what sounds trustworthy. Sort out the human greed for power and social control out of these "never to be questioned" words. Moreover, use the faculty of intuition by knowing or understanding without proof because proof you may never have. Your heart is the best filter because God loves his children. And this is the best way to reconnect with God the Father. Speak to him yourself, tell him how your heart hurts seeing all the atrocities in this hell. Tell Him about the love you have for your children, tell Him everything in a private quiet moment. These are the prayers He hears and responds to.*

*Trusting your re-connection with God to a man of religion who requires money to do this for you, should be a big red flag alarm. It is nothing more than politics and social control. No person should come between you and your Father of Heaven. Evil works to divide you from those you love and who love you. Your Earth education purpose and goal, is to identify what evil does and free yourselves from the web of lies. Be free and surround yourself by those who love you and those you love. Follow the wisdom of the words Jesus left for our moral development. Discern and grow with the lessons you learn from your life and free yourselves from all indoctrination. Be free, this is what God wishes for you to discover.*

(J. Howard, <u>The Wisdom of God,</u> Blog, 8-21-22)

# Chapter 21
# The One Called "Teacher"

*"You are in a time that does not open to many of these truths. Soon, many will speak these truths and you will hear my words in all mouths streaming like sounds of angelic voices. You are in a place of so much darkness; this is not the place for the children of God. I sent you my son and he gave you my words. Now hear my words again and take heed. The love that lives in all hearts is heard by the spiritual world, and all that hear my words will awaken to me."*

(J. Howard, <u>The Wisdom of God,</u> 2020, p. 7)


Throughout the book, God routinely calls His son, Jesus, "Teacher" as a sort of nick-name.  Whenever Jesus is mentioned, it is either about His time on Earth and His awful death or in association with Gabriel. God calls all the Archangels His sons.  Gabriel does seem to be primarily God's faithful assistant, as much as anything.  He also played big roles as mentioned in the Holy Bible as a "messenger." Jesus', or "Teacher's" role in the coming times seems to be partnered with Gabriel to bring the armies of God to stop war and begin the process of cleaning Earth and educating and reuniting the "surviving" human race.  Together they bring about the reunion of all souls.  God speaks of the events that led to Jesus' death in many parts of the book.

*"Answer to Answers" is the book that Sophia served to us before she was taken by Lucifer and used to attract many good souls to Earth. But by the time Lucifer finished with her, there was a little left of her mind and heart to be renewed. She became a believed liar, seen by these poor souls who felt betrayed by her, but she was not herself and she died soon after.*

*Because I did not know this, all stories I heard about her angered me, and all who followed her to Earth I saw as officers of evil. Because evidence of their only truth was knowledge believed by us, being corrupted, and using humans as slaves to answer to all these whores needs.*

*Then my son arrived on Earth believing he could change some of these lost souls, but he soon discovered that he was being used to again, renew the actions done to his mother. He, Christ, could not stop these waves of beliefs on Earth, and Setu truth was not shared or heard. Instead, a new religion was created to use many people looking for good in their lives, to be deceived by corrupted religious leaders who took all they desired from these poor souls.*

*These truths as shared are evident today, and you can be certain that these religious leaders are not serving truths. They have caused lies to perpetuate and their riches to expand, and nothing more renews with the people who wished to open to me."*

(J. Howard, <u>The Wisdom of God,</u> 2020, p. 7)

God was clearly angered and hurt by what happened to first, Sophia and the portion of their "family" that was captured by Lucifer, then later, the murder of Jesus.

*"See this be dealt with now, as the plan to return to Earth started when my son Jesus was murdered and changed into a cult figure. No, this was never his intention to be displayed, tortured, and dying on a cross. Who would wish for this I ask you? Who would do this to make people feel remorse for something they did not do? Is this quite clear to you now? Do you not see this as fear base actions against people who are well serving wishes of dealing with love and care for each other?*

*Know to us this is a great dishonor to be displayed like this at a moment of death. This is why this was done, and perpetuated for so long to cause us to be dealing with disrespect of who we are. And to be settling with this abomination, heels only with our truth. These whores who have done this will be judged, and actions of great punishment they will serve, as they will be serving in their right places.*

*This is justice."*

(J. Howard, <u>The Wisdom of God,</u> 2020, p. 64)

*"God gives you back your lives and your better health. Now see these times be well ended, and better serving with us, as we will help you understand the truth about your bodies, and how you will learn to heal yourselves. This was the way my son Jesus came to Earth to open this to all of you but the only response to this was martyrdom and death.*

*We do not believe in any way of martyrdom. We do not accept these ways of harming oneself in the belief that this is healing anyone or anything. All souls come to Earth to achieve evidence of great personal knowledge about who they are themselves, nothing more and nothing less. The ways of martyrdom are clearly an action to stop this process of self-knowledge and growth to become a better Setu Being and discover ways for future endeavors."*

(J. Howard, <u>The Wisdom of God,</u> 2020, p. 139)

*"Heal with us and be well served by our ways, our truth, our actions and our care. Be dealing with us, and be dealing with many more caring helps than any other seen on Earth, as we will begin to heal the sick, and the poor will have what they need.*

*These words, I shared before when my son Jesus came to Earth. Those who tortured him still display his tortured body as a sign of their own threats to you, and still, this is not understood. These demons play tricks on people and make them believe that they are all sinners. These ones are the sinners, but many people of Earth are serving without sin, and are not born with sin. Be certain of this when you see a newly born child.*

*But also understand that some are born with sin, as these whores reincarnate and answer again to their master, Lucifer. They return to his service, and renew their actions against my children, and cause again more suffering as seen as the rape of children. These actions have more to do with changing the DNA by causing anxiety, fear, and disturbances in the body than as said, as a simple rite of passage, as quoted by a catholic bishop.*

*These words are known to be the words of abusers and Lucifer, as this they do without any remorse. Evidence of remorse is not seen by these bishops and abusers of the innocent. And now all these actions of active deceptions will be soon ended, and as arrivals become seen. Be certain many will be sorted by us. Be certain those who cause harm onto others will be the first to be judged by me and my Lords."*

(J. Howard, <u>The Wisdom of God,</u> 2020, p. 228)

Johanne commented on Jesus as part of an email and had this to say on June 17, 2022:

*About Jesus, (this might not be in the book), God did not want Jesus to incarnate to Earth because He knew it would be dangerous. It was Jesus' plan to try to reunite God's children with their Father. But as we know, Lucifer is the architect of this messy world, he controls it through his whores and demons. Earth is the demon's last place in the Universes to be decontaminated.*

And in her blog, she posted these messages from God:

*" Be renewing knowledge with my son Jesus who wishes to address all with his new coming answers, but understand he heals because of his time on Earth was only brief and very troubling. Be certain bridging truth will open to many at the time of reunification and greater answers. But also see to knowledge with better answers than seen on Earth, and know we are dealing with the*

*answers to open with our way with the truth opening to many.*

*Answers are well answering many but others will be angry about giving up their power, and this helps to show all who serves whom. More comes with the war seen in the Middle-East. These wars will serve our time to open on Earth, to serve with our diplomats and our elects, who are being awakened to answer on Earth with us as we arrive.*

*Those who visit the book are seeing many truths of who we are, and are our renewed family members because all open to used (past) truths and greater seeings. However, many others who are not ready to open to truth because of the veil that serves them to answer to serving God, are seeing a god who heals only as they think and made to believe. This settles with their masters who were never chosen by me, Gabriel or Teacher (Jesus). These ones are lying to you and these ones are as the politicians who wish to control you, all your work and activities.*

*Be this said, you will see this yourselves at the time of reunification and open to many more truths about why my children are slaves on Earth, and why these demons want to vaccinate you like sick sheep when there is no knowledge about what the vaccines will open to when this settles in time with many.*

*Be certain this is only the start to their depopulation plan. Most people will be renewing with an early death or worse, living with disabilities that will be seen as responsible for further health problems like cancers, blood diseases and brain disturbances that will only serve the masters' plans to better exterminate in specific places. This will answer to evidence of an occupation from these people who wish to better themselves through the theft of land and more.*

*They want to control Earth before we arrive and rid these places of people so they can answer to us that no one will be understanding who we are at our time of truth.* **But this will not happen.** *And these whores will renew with the truth of who we are, and they will be exposed to all servants of Earth and our children.*

*See this be visited by them soon as they will try to stop us from arriving.*

*But these demons have carried on with their dealers of lies, and now many people do not trust them in evidence of believed knowledge, and soon all their lies and tricks will open to many other problems with us.*

*This is the end times for them and the evidence of beginning for us. Soon you will be answered with our greater truth. Most will understand that serving truth is responding to trust, and this my children will answer you.*

*Be certain you will be understanding how all heals with us and opens to another greater truth proving who we are and who my children are. Then we can create together a world of seeing to better days and serving trust with each other.*

*God arrives soon my children to open to your freedom and open to better ways of living on Earth with care for all responding life in the evidence of serving with all.*

*Visits come sooner now as the time heals these wars and stops further destruction the non-believers deal with in Palestine and Israel, and the seeing of who is behind this and who wants this war.*

*Be understanding we are dealing with demons who control all from their caves, and who are able to serve possessions with the weak-minded with obvious settling ways. The seen proof of possession can only be renewed as long as these beings of darkness are living, and this is what we will change by eliminating them in evidence of their crimes.*

*Soon you will see them fall one by one as this will appear as the end of a long life, but these possessions will stop and so will they. And then they will be free, well settling with what they accepted at these times of horror.*

*Be dealing with our time of greater truth, and be certain you will confirm many more seeings as we arrive.*

*Be renewed with truth only and be ready." God.*

(J. Howard, <u>The Wisdom of God,</u> Blog, 5-15-21)

And Johanne posted this on her blog as part of a larger message one day:

*Stay firm and strong in your truth, and follow Jesus' words of wisdom. He will show Himself first with Archangel Gabriel and Archangel Micheal who will stand by His side. Believe, they are my sons returning to Earth to answer back to this evil that contaminated My home thousands of your years ago.*

(J. Howard, <u>The Wisdom of God,</u> Blog, 4-12-23)

We as Christians, have been told all of our lives, the many reasons that Jesus died. They were all for us and our benefit. Let me list some of those reasons and statements:

- God sent his only son, to die for us, to remove original sin
- God sent his only son to pay for our sins
- Jesus gave his life for us to be able to enter the kingdom of heaven
- He died for the redemption of others
- Jesus died for our sins
- Jesus gave his life for us

These are some of the things that make you wonder who thought this was a "good statement to make to show how reverent you were" by claiming to be "washed in the blood of Jesus Christ or the blood of the Lamb!" What an awful image of horror. Do you not see what they do?

There was an email exchange with Johanne that I was feeling sorry for myself and was a little put off by how many times God talked about how angry He was that they murdered His son. I thought to myself, why would He be so upset, because after death, He got his son back. I thought "my son died also, but I didn't get him back, at least not yet.

# Chapter 22
# Incarnations

Incarnations and reincarnations are frequent subjects spoken of in the book, **The Wisdom of God.**

I have thought about this many times throughout my life. Once I watched a video about children who had real life experiences where they recalled a different time they had lived. The video spoke of how children in the 3- to 7-year-old age groups seem to frequently recall what could only be explained as "former lives", claiming that they remembered these other times, when they were someone else. One young boy in the video in that age range, said something to his parents about when he lived in another nearby town. They took the opportunity to quiz him for more details. He described being old, married and living in a particular house which he described. He talked about his wife and other simple things. One day the parents took him for a drive to see if they could find the house he described as his old home.  They found a home and he said it was his.  They went to the door, knocked and were greeted by an older woman that the boy claimed was his former wife.  I don't remember all the details after that, but it shocked all the adults and it reaffirmed my thoughts that we do have some sort of reincarnation process we exist in.  Most of the time, adults just let it go and don't give it more thought, when a young child says something incredible like that.  I have a story within our family that relates to this.  I wrote about the event to Johanne, to get her thoughts on it.  As part of the email I sent on November 13th 2022, I said:

> *I have a quick little story for you..........We had one of Nana's little granddaughters for an overnight stay a couple of days ago.  She is named JoJo and is the sweetest little thing.  She is the one, if you recall, that I told of that had asked her mommy if they could pray for the people in the ambulance that had just passed by them.  That was when she was three.  She is now four.  Anyway, Nana told me they were talking as they were working on some craft projects at the table.  She had asked Nana about doing something and Nana said that she would need to be older, whatever it was that she wanted to do.  She replied, "I was 10 once." This took Nana by surprise and asked her what she meant by that.  She never said anything more about*

*"that". She said, "when I was coming this time, I saw how good my mommy I have now could be, so I chose her"……………what do you think about that?? I told Nana I wish I had been there as I could have really played that out and asked more questions. You know, over time, I have heard similar stories come out of kids about that age; 3-5 years old. That seems to be the age. I watched a YouTube video once that had about 10 different stories of little ones talking about past lives with great accuracy.*

She responded the next day:

*I believe in children remembering their past lives. It makes sense to me that the heart memory carries the soul memory. The brain is the engineer and the heart is the conductor. Also measured by a cardiologist medical engineer (name?) with a similar instrument used by Dr Valerie Hunt. He said his instrument could only measure 8 meters of the energy field but he believed the heart can extend up to across the Earth. There is so much we don't know. It reminds me of the pictures of the Holy Mother and Jesus with their hearts shining outward.*

An email exchange we had about Jesus on July 27th of 2023 started with this thought about death, about my son's death and God's reactions to Jesus' death:

*It has stuck in my mind the words God used in your book and I believe you also wrote in a blog sometime that, God was angry that they "murdered His son, Jesus." As a father who has lost a son, I have felt anger too, from being "robbed" of my time with him. I feel he was "taken" from me..........*

*But, a few days ago, I had the thought again, about how God was angered by His murder, to which suddenly, I said to myself, "why would he be so angry?" Did Jesus not raise a few days later in that same body and now is with God? I am still angry that my son was taken from me, because unlike God, mine is not with me. It is so confusing. I do not understand the anger that His human life was ended when almost immediately, He was returned. It must have been a horrific beating and death. Thousands, probably, have suffered the same death in those days and other times since. I think I read somewhere that God said Jesus still suffers today from the effects of the beatings. That tells me it was more than just a physical attack but an attack on his very soul, on the life and spirit within.*

To which she replied and spoke of the incarnation of Jesus and what led up to that:

> *You answered your own questions about why God is angry for what they did to his son. The way I understand this is God did not want Jesus to go to Earth. Primarily, Jesus wanted to try to awaken/save his mother. Mary's soul was so tormented and abused life after life, she never knew who she was. Lucifer torments people to imprint fear and pain, and especially he abused the Mother so she could never return home and take her place by God's side. She is the missing being, the Holy Spirit of the Trinity. God did not agree with Jesus' plan. Jesus has free will and decided to incarnate as the son of Mary.*

In the book, **<u>The Wisdom of God</u>**, several passages talk of the cycle of incarnations that occur. "Normal" incarnations were meant to be a series of life experiences that built upon one another over time, to accumulate knowledge and to improve oneself. Lucifer changed that and all memories of past lives began to be forgotten, so lessons were never learned. Humans were kept in a slave type process, to keep serving the dark ones in an eternal, never ending cycle.

God explained this in these messages:

*"With these words, I wish to tell you that death is not as you see on Earth. On Earth, the body is used until completion, and then the soul returns to answer to another life. Be renewing this knowledge with us, and see how these ways were manipulated to erase all soul memories, to have another control of your destiny, and outcome of your lives. Renewing with this may be difficult to accept, as you have all accepted the facts of aging and death. Be surprised to know these ways only exist on Earth as you are being used as slaves to serve these demons. Be certain you will soon be free of these many returns to different lives, as the truth will open you to this knowledge."*

(J. Howard, <u>The Wisdom of God</u>, 2020, p.23,24)

*"Understand that it is darkness that imprisoned you on Earth, and it is light from your creator that has come to free you from eternal reincarnation.*

*Death is a gateway to the place called Heaven. This place is an island of coming shared knowledge of the greatest love. This place holds all beings accountable for their choices on Earth. Answer to only those who dwell in this place."*

(J. Howard, <u>The Wisdom of God</u>, 2020, p.6)

*"Many years later, we were sending Scouts to visit the near planets to be seeing to stories of great changes on Earth. Be seeing why we are here and only now. Understand the uses for incarnations served to adapt to*

*other planets atmospheres, and better serving answers to many more uses of physical realities. Better serving these methods we devised to question our time of living history to be well serving of our ways of evolution and growing knowledge.*

*These ways were taken by the alien Lucifer, who wanted to create an answer to manipulating human bodies, and causing aging under a genetic method used by his beings' kind only. These ways, as seen on Earth, stops a good person from experiencing their evolution as it repeats the sequences of life with no resolution, and nothing opens to them."*

(J. Howard, <u>The Wisdom of God</u>, 2020, p.42,43)

God explained that when they discovered what was happening on Earth, they rushed back to their home and found themselves in somewhat of an ambush and the great heavenly war erupted.

*"But soon the wars began with the demon Reptilians, and we only settled to escape at the seeing of great numbers. They attacked us with great strength, and we did not know of these kinds before, so we needed to outpost on another planet to try to settle with our defeat. These times were necessary for us to regain power over our time of truth and strength was served to us by the elders or Ancient Ones who explained to us that our strength needed to be unified.*

> *Soon all others joined with us to answer to our unification under the Setu seeing of the Universal Laws, and we became well serving together more than expected. The Ancient Ones told us of the seeing on Earth and how now was the time to return and reclaim our planet, given the situation of possible destruction."*

(J. Howard, <u>The Wisdom of God</u>, 2020, p.200)

As I understand how Lucifer's system worked, they had to "dumb down" humans by "unhooking" some of the DNA connections and creating a sort of "magnetic grid" that captured souls, stopping them from returning to source or Heaven. This allowed the dividing of souls and the reuse of souls without their memory functions. A blog post alluded to this by this statement:

> *"Be certain now all opens to better days, and be certain many will serve with greater seen truth as we are and as we wish to be. Visits are opening soon and we will dismantle the grid made to cage the servants of God. And we will begin to remove all those who are escaping the humans' grasps of people who are in the service of Lucifer's dark ways of death, in evidence of those who cannot be changed."*

(J. Howard, <u>The Wisdom of God</u>, Blog, 1-25-22)

# Chapter 23
# Our Immortal Souls

What is a soul?  Is it a being, a spirit, or is it life?

I talked at length with my wife about it and decided to discuss it with Johanne and maybe get some divine help to understand the process.  I emailed her on August 18, 2022:

*Johanne,*

*I have a question (a subject with several questions actually) that I think about from time to time.  It is about the soul.*

*I have always believed that the soul is the very "life" that is in everything.  No dead thing can have a soul or life in it, so when life leaves, the vessel contains no soul. All mammals must have souls. Does plant life? Maybe a different kind of soul?*

*One day recently, I came upon the thought that, in humans especially, the soul must be, besides a spirit form, a being in itself. If it is an individual (as a being), does it have an identifier, a name or something that it is called, no matter in what life form it resides? I understand it as primarily energy, but it must have a physical life form, I would think. So, it is spiritual and it is physical. It has a desire to learn and experience "being" through living in different "bodies." It probably can be killed or be "ended" by forces greater than we know. Its beginning must have been part of original creation and has a duty or mission to gain knowledge and develop its character, through reincarnations. From what I can imagine, the Angels must have souls also, or maybe they are a higher form of souls.*

*All of these questions came to me as I was wondering if I could "contact" my soul. I wondered if my soul has a "name" that it might recognize as being called to communicate. Then I thought that I am who the soul is, so it would be like me trying to get Mike's attention to talk. "First person to first person" doesn't work as far as I know. In your book, God said to develop our ability to communicate with Him, we had to open up our hearts. He also explained that it is in our hearts that our souls live, our spirit, our life force. That has me a bit confused in that I don't think I have an open communication with God (doesn't seem to be) which led me to wondering if I have to get in touch with my soul somehow to form communication with it, to open to God. Complicated, I know, but that's how I got to wondering about the soul being, kind of, a separate being from me and must have an identifier (name). I also have a problem understanding the concept of the split souls; souls residing in multiple bodies. That is another thing I don't want to get into as it also adds complication.*

*You can probably tell; I have too much time on my hands these days! (lol)*

*Have a lovely day!*

*Mike Maher*

On August 20<sup>th</sup>, Johann answered my email with this:

*Good morning, Mike,*

*I hope you and your family are doing all very well and in good health.*

*I will try to answer your question but I don't know all the answers of course. I too am on a path of learning, so this is what I learned so far about the soul. The soul is essentially you. Your soul is on a mission to learn and develop, travelling in body life after life, reincarnation.*

*Souls on Earth are at many different levels of learning. Some are done with this Earth education and move on to the next place (?) and I have no real knowledge of what that can be like. I believe we are in a "bad school" because the chancellor is Lucifer, making this a chaos and a hell for many souls.*

*MK ultra victims are said to have fragmented personalities from extreme abuses, usually started at a young age. A fragmented soul suffers the same treatment and can only survive if it is fragmented into many bodies in one present life. But I cannot know this for certain, this is what I understand. So, this divided/fragmented soul is not complete and cannot complete its learning mission and Earthly experiences from Earth as was meant to be.*

*Some people seem to be without a soul. There is no depth to their thinking and actions. Those may be fragments, and what is seen is a piece of a soul that needs to be discarded. These pieces are easily possessed by demons. These pieces cannot return to the Heavens and will no longer exist after this life. It is like a refining process. The best of the soul will survive with God's healing. Lucifer needs fragments to continue to exist.*

*In a recent message (not shared), God said "have no tears for these ones when they leave". To us they seem like a full person but this person is not a full soul, and thus serves the "architect of the world" Lucifer.*

*On a lighter note, I put this on the wall of my shed to remind me of the macro view of life, the bigger picture. And I find #4 to be especially relevant for me because I knew this before I found this page. I could see experiences repeating themselves becoming stronger until I got it.*

*Here is Your Assignment…*

*1. You Will Receive A Body*
*You may like it or not, but it will be yours for the entire period this time around.*

*2. You Will Learn Lessons.*
*You are enrolled in a full-time, informal school called life. Each day in this school you will have the opportunity to learn lessons. You may like the lessons or think them irrelevant and stupid.*

*3. There Are No Mistakes, Only Lessons.*
*Growth is a process of trial and error, experimentation. The "failed" experiments are as much a part of the process as the experiment that ultimately "Works."*

*4. A Lesson is Repeated Until it is Learned.*
*A lesson will be presented to you in various forms until you have learned it, then you can go onto the next lesson.*

*5. Learning Lessons Does Not End.*
*There is no part of life that does not contain its*
*lessons. If you are alive, there are lessons to be learned.*

*6. "There" is no better than "Here".*
*When your "there" has become "here", you will simply*
*obtain another "there" that will, again, look better*
*than "here".*

*7. Others are Merely Mirrors of You.*
*You cannot love or hate something about another*
*person unless it reflects to you something you love or*
*hate about yourself.*

*8. What You Make of Your Life is Up to YOU.*
*You have all the tools and resources you need, what*
*you do with them is up to you. The choice is yours.*

*9. All Answers Lie Inside You.*
*The answers to life's question lie inside you. All you*
*need to do is look, listen, and trust.*

*10. Whether You Think You Can or Can't,*
*In Either Case You'll Be Right.*
*Think about it.*

*Author Unknown*

*How to open your heart to God? For me it was when*
*I questioned all of education (I was a high school teacher*
*for 20 years), and I was seeing how superficial and*
*damaging it was to children. Then one day at around*
*6pm, I went shopping and waited for a woman and her*

*child to finish their choices at a dairy section. The boy was no more than 5 years old wearing a school uniform with a jacket, tie and black shoes. The mother was wearing a suit and heels. The child responded to the mother's thoughts, he was able to read her mind and she harshly said to him "I did not say anything", and he mildly said she did. My heart painfully opened to an understanding. When I went home, I wrote a letter to God asking why people are so cruel to their own children, and why wasn't that child at home playing or outside getting fresh air. This mother had more on her mind than her own child. This is when I began to get answers and started to communicate. It was Uriel who spoke to me first and did for many months, then Raphael and later Micheal, Gabriel and God. And my true education began with them as they guided what I needed to see and understand. My whole world exploded.*

*Years later in our neighborhood, a local High School student was found by his mother hanging from a backyard tree. I wondered if it was the same boy.*

*Take care, talk to God or the Angels.*

*Johanne*

I answered back the same day:

*Hi Johanne,*

*Thank you for sharing your wisdom regarding my queries. I read your message to Nana and we followed up with a "deep" discussion, attempting to gain some kind of understanding between us, recognizing good souls and evil souls amongst those close to us.*

*I'm not sure I have shared this story with you. About 30 years ago, I had the opportunity to give a US Senator a tour of our manufacturing facility. I don't remember exactly why I was given the honor of leading the tour, but I was. At one point, I engaged in a one-on-one conversation with the politician without the others being involved, as he had questions and focused on me and my "knowledge." As I discussed things with him, face to face, I realized as I looked in his eyes, that there was nothing there!! Honestly, I didn't know what to think. He was talking intelligently with me, but I could see no "life" or "thinking" in those eyes. It shocked me so much, I confided in another friend who met him also, that this happened and he said the same thing. The look of emptiness behind his eyes. I now think that he had no soul! Lots of things you bring to us either personally, or on your blog, or in your book, resonates with many of my life experiences. I have come to use you as a sounding board to help me decide what I need to do to keep on the right path and to learn from the experiences that I have recorded in memory but have not gotten answers to the "what was that?" or the "why did that happen?" Thank you for taking my first questions and continuing to communicate with me.*

*God has blessed us and provided us a connection through you.*

*Your friends,*

*Mike and Nana*

Johanne entered on her blog, this message from God and additional notes about souls in January 2024:

*"Seeing us arrive will be the proof of our strength and numbers, greater than any armies on Earth. All who believe their armies are greater have more to discover as we arrive. Be amazed by these numbers coming, we will settle with all those who are corrupted.*

*A long time ago, we were all united until these days ended with the arrival of these demons who began renewing with us as friends, served with us and lied to us about their power and abilities. Lucifer settled with us because he was from another planet. We thought he was a survivor and accepted his presence amongst us.*

*He learned many of our ways but was only seen as another visitor learning of our truths. Soon he became another, helping only himself and wanting to change the way of sharing our truth, and then he used our answers to open to a greater problem.*

*Lucifer went to another part of Earth, where he began experimenting with others and created beasts like dinosaurs to destroy our world. Be understanding, all the troubles used to stop us. These large animals terrorized us and opened to great troubles of survival, as we did not know where these creatures came from, and certainly how we could remove them.*

*This became another problem as these beings were soulless and aggressive, destroying all in their path. But only a few of us were able to escape. And those who did not were captured and made to be different through many changes, only to be lesser than his own followers.*

*This is why you are seeing this be repeated on Earth at this time, with the DNA being changed by vaccines and worse drugs to attack the nervous system, destroying all semblance to the being that should be. In response to these manipulations, are shorter lives that cannot function independently but responds only to slavery and death.*

*Only those who suffer through this will know that they are being duped to answer to more deadly treatment that responds to their extermination. Then, all who trusted these doctors who are setting with lies, are coerced to answer to another vaccine or drug.*

*These doctors are settling with answers to an early death. And they care not who or what these patients are.*

*Another truth opens to why they are doing this. They themselves are broken souls who were changed by Lucifer's work. They are only serving the lies they were told. These lies only renew with deadly troubles of health going wrong, they believe they are helping the victim and see only this.        These doctors are fragmented souls who believe they are helpful. Many are this way and some are not. Now you are seeing this, and because you know my words, you are conscious of how all opens and serve with better answers.*

*Be visited by our time of better renewals, and seeing to our good doctors, who, as said, will arrive to help those who were coerced and forced to comply. And at this time of great renewal, we will heal all who are bridging with us and opening to our ways of healing.*

*These times are near and open to greater times than seen on Earth, proving many of our truths, our ways and shared believed knowledge".*

*God My notes:  (Johanne)*

*Fragmented souls are beings who are not complete and who are unable to see anything differently of what is presented to them within their limits of ability and understanding. They are capable of functioning within a compartmentalized, structured system, but cannot think outside the box and have difficulty in creative and critical thinking.*

*They often repeat what they are told to the letter. Furthermore, they cannot hear or listen to any other possibility because it does not fit within their reality. They are as pieces of a being that exists as part of a hive-mind, and these beings' souls were prepared through many abused lives to respond to a certain directive and specific tasks.  They appear to be sometimes very personable and friendly; however, it is nothing more than an acquired, learned response.*

*Not only that, but they pretend to hear you, as if to play along with what is expected, prescribed behavior, but they cannot understand another opinion or concern and secure themselves in arrogance and often hidden disregard for others. Likewise, they may appear as experts in their field, but they are, in fact, deaf and blind to the truth of others realities and lives. What we understand to be psychopaths or sociopaths are these fragmented souls who have no consciousness. It is a disconnect from the spiritual world and God, as their light is dim or non-existent.*

*During the sorting time, these beings will be removed and put in a place where they can heal and evolve, no matter how long it will take. Presently, many of these beings are here on Earth in greater numbers, reincarnated to serve the purpose of participating in the destruction of Earth at the service of Lucifer.*

*There are also those who are aggressive criminals who are completely soulless and aware of their evil actions, possessed by another force or demon, and who take pleasure in causing harm and deaths. Moreover, others are 'backdrop beings' who play a role in the world without any conscious thought and function as slaves trying to survive and serve a master.*

*All of these beings will be put in their right place to be healed, and to be helped in their evolution.*

*Be one with God*

(J. Howard, The Wisdom of God, Blog, 1-17-24)

In another email in March of 2024, I had these thoughts I passed on to Johanne about the characteristics of a soul, the physical nature of it:

> *Along the lines of incarnations, I have wondered about the characteristics of a soul. For instance, if a soul is a lifeform, then how big or small is it? If it resides in the heart, then I have questions about that. Starting with conception, how does a soul fit into a two celled embryo? Does a soul, possibly, not enter a body until it has a working heart? A heart forms in a fetus in the 4th to 6th week, then starts pumping blood. The fetus has life before that because it is taking in nutrients and growing, changing and forming a body with DNA directions. If a soul is life, then the soul should be there from minute number one, in the development of the fetus. OR, could the soul reside "outside" of the body, invisibly, but directly attached, therefore being able to be any size it needs to be, no matter what the size of the body it is attached to. When two sets of DNA are joined into one child being, does a part of the soul of each parent reside to that soul?*

Johanne was busy during the next few days, helping her sister and we never went back and rehashed the subjects I had brought up. I still wonder about these things.

On April 30,2025 Johann posted on her blog the following information about fragmented souls.

*God uses words that we currently use in our own languages to communicate with us. The languages people use on Earth are not the language of the Angels. Telepathy and vibration is their way of communication. On Earth, we have some of these abilities that are disregarded and discouraged at an early age. Still, many people share their precognition experiences. As a small example, knowing who will be contacting you before it happens, or dreaming of an event that comes later, like déjà vu. And then, there are people who never have these experiences and who do not dream. This is what is called a fragmented soul being or an empty vessel.*

*These beings are only guided by impulses and conditioning. Not everyone walking has a soul with the ability to act with empathy or compassion. Modern science tries to explain this phenomenon through personality disorders and psychological conditions.*

*Some individuals lack the divine spark that makes us fully human. As children, my sister and I would identify people as shark eyes or dead eyes, and by this we meant they had no kindness in them, and were not trustworthy. The soul is what makes us truly human. The "anima" explained by many philosophers like Aristotle, and more recently by Jung, is the inner self, the soul, connects to the divine light. For some, this divine light is dimmed or inexistent, which makes a person act without guilt, remorse or genuine empathy. They respond with acquired social responses learned from others. These people have no dreams or do not remember dreams.*

*Some of these empty vessels are not necessarily evil, but they lack moral compass and spiritual connection. Still, the soul can evolve.*

*What is considered an empty vessel or a soulless being could be a being who has not yet awaken to their soul's evolutionary journey. In modern neuroscience, researchers' observations and studies of consciousness has identified states of people, who appear fully functional, but lack emotional resonance or moral intuition. Also, think about Stanley Milgram's (1960's) experiment, where 65% of participants administered the maximum shock level despite hearing the hidden learners' distress by order of the authority figure demands.*

*These explanations give us the opportunity to look at those who appear as empty vessels or fragmented souls, with compassion. They may awaken to their soul's potentiality during the journey of the soul.*

*Many Earthly experiences can prevent a soul to fully attain it's potential, making it appear as a soulless being. This can be caused by trauma, neurological conditions, or environmental influences, much alike living in constant survival mode. All these elements can be what appears as an absence of soul. In reality, we are possibly facing a soul temporarily prevented from fully manifesting.*

*In the study of epigenetics, we observe that traumatic experiences can alter gene expression across generations, affecting behaviors without changing fundamental DNA, and therefore these behaviors become innate knowledge. This could explain why children living in a safe and comfortable environment can suffer from depression and anxiety.*

*This is all part of the developmental stages of a soul's evolution. Some can be very young souls on the road to development. Dehumanizing those who think differently causes extreme polarization and divisiveness. Recognizing the divine spark and potential in everyone is the first step towards true spiritual evolution. This does not mean in any way to accept evil and the acts of evil. People say "I will pray for them", which means so they can see the light and evolve, hopefully in this life.*

(J. Howard, The Wisdom of God, Blog, 4-30-25)

# Chapter 24
# Alien God

One morning, when I was getting dressed and ready for my day, there came suddenly, the thought of writing this book. For many years I had considered doing some writing, but had never decided what the subject would be. This particular morning, I realized a path to this. I thought, "Of course, this would be a great way to tell this story" And I went about my day with no other thought of it. The very next morning, it suddenly became a thought again, and I realized I had forgotten and this was my reminder. Very quickly, I could visualize a cover and on it said, "Alien God," without any more need for reminders, I now had a mission to accomplish.

# Alien God

In 2014, Johann noted in her book,

> *On April 6, I received a message from my contact, alien/angel called God, (I write this with no intention of disrespect,) he said, "be ready and be dealing with the better serving truth starting soon as the North Koreans are responding to rage about the murder of their leader's character with the image sent by Anonymous. And this is how we will answer back to them with our time to walk the Earth."*
>
> *Like all of you from all places in the world who are reading these messages, I have no way of knowing anything for certain. All I can wish and hope for is that these Beings are truthful and they're coming here for the reasons that I have stated. It would be amazing to better the lives of people on Earth.*

(J. Howard, *The Wisdom of God,* 2020, p282)

> *Evidence of their actions will determine how their actions will be dealt with. But for now, we only see these days as well serving. All have free will, and although we are seen as Aliens, we are actually Setu Beings of Light returning to our own created planet. See our arrivals has more than uses of an invasion, but the understood truth of our return. Know we are soon here with you.*

J. Howard, *The Wisdom of God,* 2020, p54)

*Know, now this. The way of the telling of who we are as Beings of Light may seem as untrue to most, as the stories on Earth renewed with a great lie of who we are and the way our children were cared for by us we are called 'gods of renowned', but we are in many ways as human in our looks. Be not surprised by this, and be ready to see how we are answering to our own, and how now is the time to awaken into these coming seen truths.*

*We have been on Earth many times before, and we have caused some of the great cataclysms to heal the problems with the Annunaki and their creation of monsters as the seen dinosaurs. But we are not the Annunaki and until we knew who they are, we could not deal with them and their renewed dealings of destruction of planets as they stole and took whatever they wanted to answer to their desires of control.*

(J. Howard, <u>The Wisdom of God,</u> 2020, p124)

*Who I am is healing your seeing of our arrivals. Many have the belief that God is a mystical being who created Earth in seven days. These words are a creation of Lucifer, who wanted to reduce you to fear me and control your beliefs. This heals as we will make our presence known on Earth and then you can decide for yourselves what you need to open to as all is revealed. Be serving your truth, this is all I can ask you to open to, and then see the rest unravel.*

*Now many have asked me where I come from. We are living now on a large ship as big as the moon ship. Be certain all these truths will soon be well shared, and well explained as we arrive and show you these truths. How we made our ships and our pyramids are all things we will share with you as we removed the demons who have well concealed themselves on Earth in bodies and who will open to these times with our way of removing them.*

(J. Howard, <u>The Wisdom of God,</u> 2020, p150)

*When God, Jesus, Gabriel, Micheal, Uriel and the many others arrive, the powers that be will tell you it is a lie and not to believe these "Aliens". They will tell you they want to take over the governments and create their own world. They will say this because they themselves served darkness and have much to fear. After everything I have learnt, I will not trust anything the government wants me to believe. I serve with God. God is my Father.*

*These Beings of Light will cause the many who serve darkness to be removed; either by their own destructive actions against each other, by their own hand, or by the Beings' actions against this evil. No stone will be left unturned, as God said. So, of course evil will tell all that God and the Angels are a trick, an enemy, a take-over and spin it to their advantage and cause more fear. Do not be afraid. Lift up your hearts and spirits, and rise up children of God.*

(J. Howard, <u>The Wisdom of God</u>, Blog, Mar 2, 2013)

And here I am.  This is not the God I was taught about as a child and believed most of my adult life, but it all makes perfect sense to me after all I have read and experienced now in my time.  Where else would He and the Angels be from?  They must live up there somewhere, be it in a place we call heaven or maybe on a ship temporarily, that has a destination of Earth, which perhaps, is the true Heaven or Garden of Eden. He does describe this as a reason for creating Earth, as a place to come and relax, much like a vacation destination. He also describes it as their home, a place of comfort.   I do not have contact such as Johanne Howard does.  I have asked a few times in prayer, since all of this began, but it may not be my place to be in contact.  And, I am okay with that.   Johanne is very protective of her gift and I have always respected her for that.  She tries to be a conduit of God's words, not a filter.  I have no doubt that the day they come, there will be sheer terror and chaos.  The ones that know this is coming, like you are now, will be essential to the calming of the masses.  I expect that you have read these words and know that it may be your place to help others.  To calm fears.  To gently explain that now should be a time to rejoice and to be grateful that you got to be one of the chosen, to be here for this.  To witness the return of our God and his son Jesus.

# Chapter 25
# Be Ready;
# All Comes as I Said

"Be Ready, all comes as I said" ………Many times I read those words written by Johanne at the end of a chapter in her book, as it is repeated in several places. "Trust me and what I say is the Truth," would be the general meaning.  At the end of every chapter in <u>The Wisdom of God</u>, it has either a short directive like that or just God, then, received by Za and the date of that message.   Part of being ready is being physically prepared. In the book, God suggests we have supplies such as food, water, and medicines to stay in our homes for a couple of weeks, during their arrivals. That is good advice anytime.   It is called disaster or emergency planning, in business terms.  If I think about it, her whole book of messages is somewhat preparing us for what is to come. To awaken us, to give us background knowledge, telling us what to look for such as the signs of the times, the wars and specific activities that will open to the final conflict. **Just Be Ready**.

None of this series of coming events would have happened had it not been for Sophia writing her book and explaining what was the right way to live a peaceful existence and warning us of the evil that Lucifer brought. It is such a vast story that has lasted thousands of years and began before the time of Jesus, before the time of Noah and the great flood, before the books of the Bible, before anything we know about God and the Angels. This book was written possibly millions of years ago. This is the great story about God creating Earth and a peaceful place for living. Then Lucifer comes along, deceives these peaceful "Setu" Beings, claiming he had a new idea for "enhancing" the life experience here and they trusted him. At the time, they didn't know yet that he had a history of destroying other planets in the same way as we are seeing ours being ravaged now through wars and pollution. He started his changing of Earth and the inhabitants to create a slave population, with a cycle of reincarnations that are never ending. Sophia tried to stop him, was captured and eventually placed into that same incarnation system. Reading Johanne's book, you learn about the long process our immortal souls normally would go through to gain knowledge and understanding through many lives lived, but retaining the lessons learned.  Lucifer used a system that took those memories away through each reincarnation, so the soul never "remembered."  This passage from the book, <u>The Wisdom of God</u>, explains best, about Sophia's book:

*"Answer to Answers" is the book of truth about how all came to be, as these words written by my beloved Sophia were found out much later than dealt with by her. She knew about the unraveling of Lucifer's ways, but healing with this was only renewing with us much later as I believed she left to be used by Lucifer with consent.*

*Later Gabriel found these words in the place we call the Akashic Records where all books are kept, and the Archangel who governs this place, gave these words to Gabriel. He read them and shared these words with me. And here I discovered the erasing of cosmic memories, and the slaves reported to be serving Lucifer.*

*We are beings of choice and freedom. We did not see how these ways were settling, and we learned about these ways as we began to unravel evil ways. We informed others from other planets and soon we had a great plan to stop this by sharing together, these words left by her.*

(J. Howard, <u>The Wisdom of God</u>, 2020, P.183)

Reading those words, you see the sudden realization God had that Sophia had not left Him to go follow Lucifer, which had greatly saddened Him. He understood that He needed to embark on a rescue mission to save her and "us," caught up in this awful slavery system.  God tried a few things to solve this problem including a great flood, but that didn't stop it. This is what brought Jesus to incarnate as another plan He had, to try to awaken the mother.  Then, He was "discovered" and eventually, murdered.  There came a time, I'm not sure when, but both God and Lucifer knew how all this ends and this is what is written in the book of Revelation.  Lucifer still thinks he can outwit the Angels and has a plan to create a massive death event, releasing many souls at once and stealing away with them to another place, before God and His army can stop them.

From the Blog written August 20, 2024:

*Messages, August 20, 2024: Israel and Iran.*

*"The bomb they are sending will kill millions of people. And then, many will be settling with these ways of death in the following many days. Nothing can stop this destruction. And all who see these days will understand the truth of my words and warnings.*

*This comes before we land. And then, all better truth will begin to answer many, as these days settle with greater serving trust in answers to shared knowledge and more. Now be with us in evidence of these coming days, and settle with Earth ways.*
*Better to see all shared knowledge with us."* God
(J. Howard, *The Wisdom of God*, Blog, 8/20/24)

And another message about a massive event was part of a blog message on September 26, 2024:

*This starts in October, and will renew after an attack is launch in the USA, better settling with Iran in evidence of Israel settling with them because they are renewing with the head of the beast. This launching of a nuclear war, renewed by the Islamists, opens the way for many beliefs of a god coming to stop this. But we will not stop this first attack because these Universal Laws settle with these acts of destruction, not intent.*

*And then we will arrive to better serve these ends of wars and the removal of evil on Earth. North Korea will try to launch missiles at the seeing of the USA being attacked, but they will be stopped, and all others will be stopped from further destruction.*

*This understood answer will open to our arrivals, and we will open the way for great healing, truth with knowledge that will serve all who are believing in truth. And at these great moments of reunification, all will become changed.*

This will be the moment that brings them.  God said to Johanne that we would know about the book Sophia wrote, at or by, the time this event happens.  He started dictating the book to Za many months ago but stopped with her getting only about 5 pages of notes.  She has questioned him about when they could resume, but nothing has been said again.  What she had, she shared with me on a phone call one day and it described in Sophia's words, her being held in a cage, in a dark place underground and was being tormented without end.  She was pleading with God to rescue her and the rest of God's children but he wouldn't answer.  It was a highly emotionally charged situation and Johanne had a hard time reading it to me as well.  We don't know what the book will say but it will come eventually.  My belief is that it will be written by then and we will know.

# Chapter 26
# Awakening

We all have life within us.  That life is our soul.  That soul is immortal or at least it lasts longer than we can even imagine.  It is more than intelligence.  It has great power and abilities we cannot comprehend.  Our human life form must have a source, a place that it originates and is connected to.  That source is God.  The heart is where the soul lives and the DNA in our system is the creation of God.

My experiences the last six years have greatly affected my spiritual foundation and have expanded the possibilities and the satisfaction of the new understandings, that I hold dearly now.  The God I have always believed in, is still my God.  He is still our Creator.  He wishes to have a relationship with us and prefers a conversation over ritualistic or traditional prayers. Like Johanne has said to me so many times, ask God to put something in our path to help us understand. Ask for assistance through understanding and learning lessons.

Our beliefs about God and the Angels are all based on what has been written in the Holy Books. These writers of those books, lived thousands of years before us and the technology we now possess. As a human race, we know so much more in these days and with the help of that technology imagining Beings living outside of our Earthly confines is not much of a stretch of the imagination now. What I have presented to you here has only been small parts and basic foundational understandings that I needed to realize how this could be happening. Johanne gracefully answered all my questions as she could and when she couldn't, she asked for divine assistance and you experienced here how that was accomplished.

Anyone who knows me personally, knows that I ask many questions. I am always looking to know more. In this story, you saw the many ways I tried to approach things, all meant to help me believe what I was hearing and seeing. I still have many questions and you have read here these words, *"Question me face to face **Mike** because we have much to share together."* That statement slowed me down a bit, but if I wonder about something, I do continue to ask.

Johanne and I continue to communicate through emails and an occasional phone call or text but the intensity has lessened over time and we now talk about our gardens or such things these days. When we see something in the news that gets our attention, we know what is happening and what it brings one day. We share our thoughts on all significant world events and sometimes about things that happen within our families or where we live.

Recently, she was approached by a former student, who is a teacher now and a voice actor, wondering if Johanne would consider doing an audio book. "Irina" offered to read and record the book, _The Wisdom of God_. So, it was done in chapters and Johanne's sister, created a YouTube channel and posted the entire book on it. The YouTube channel is called, _Messages from our Father God._ Irina is originally from Russia, where they are taught English but it is British English style, so she has a British English and Russian accent. She reads in a way that you will understand the book's messages far clearer than what I was experiencing in my many times reading the book. As you recall, I mentioned that I tried to read it by remembering the accents the Russian folks used, that I had met before. It made the book easier to read for me. I also found it a bit ironic that the Russian accent would enter into the picture many years later. I suggest reading the book while listening to Irina as she reads the messages. The blog that

Johanne continues, is easily found under the heading, The Wisdom of God  at godcallshischildren.ca/blog.


Bring yourself forward in time to these days and these current times we live in and with a new "set of eyes". Consider the possibilities and see if this is the truth you seek when you think of how all came to be and why the world is the way it is.  I understand how it is easy to be skeptical. We all have been raised and lived in our established religious system.

This was my story of what I had to consider as I processed this information.  How I had to reconsider all of my spiritual beliefs.  I do not ask anyone to just believe what I have written here, but to weigh my words using your heart and intuition.  Then, if you trust your soul and your feelings, prepare to meet our Alien God.

## About the Author

Michael Maher was born and educated in South Dakota. He was raised on farms and as the oldest grandchild, was able to work with grandparents there in their later years. Conversations with Grandparents led to a lifelong love of exploring the family history and genealogy. Along with siblings, he was raised in the Catholic faith. With his questioning character he wondered about general religious beliefs, customs and differences between religious organizations. Through an amazing connection he set out to find his own truth about who we are and about source.

An avid archer for most of his life, Michael became a competitive shooter for several decades. His work career, although starting with a farm background, went from construction to manufacturing quickly. He began a long career with a major window and door manufacturer. Starting in assembly processes, then into inventory control, warehousing, trucking and distribution. The last years before retiring, he was the Director of Distribution and Logistics, managing the process from taking finished product through regional storage and final delivery to customers.

Today, Michael enjoys using his skills of cheese making, processing maple syrup, gardening, food preservation with canning, drying and freezing methods. Many skills that he was taught by his grandparents. Cooking has become a favorite pastime. He is a father and a grandfather, a brother, a cousin and an uncle to many. One on one conversations with his children and grandchildren are his most joyful moments. And, everybody gets hugs!